CONTENTS

Professional Golf Management (PGM) Flashcard Review Book

Flashcards for PGM Levels 1, 2, and 3

Level 1 Flashcards 1

Level 2 Flashcards 127

Level 3 Flashcards 227

Index 331

Professional Golf Management (PGM) Flashcard Review Book

Comprehensive Flashcards for PGM Levels 1, 2, and 3

Written by
Ryan Brandeburg, PGA
Matthew Brandeburg, CFP

A publication of
Coventry House Publishing

Copyright © 2013 Coventry House Publishing

All rights reserved.

ISBN: 0615788017
ISBN-13: 978-0615788012

LEVEL 1

Swing Weight

Adjusting Swing Weight

Swing Weight

- Definition: Measure of a golf club's moment of inertia at a particular point
- Influences the overall feel and playing characteristics of a golf club
- Two primary factors that affect swing weight are the length of the shaft and mass of the clubhead
- For every 1 inch of length that is added to a driver, the swing weight will increase by 6 points
- If swing weight is too heavy, the shaft will become too flexible

---

Adjusting Swing Weight

- Adjust swing weight by adding or removing weight from the clubhead
- To decrease swing weight, drill holes in the clubhead or hosel
- To increase swing weight, add lead tape to the lowest portion of the clubhead
- Avoid counterbalancing as a method of adjusting swing weight

Counterbalancing

———————

**Relationship Between
Shaft Flexibility & Clubhead Weight**

Counterbalancing

- Definition: Decreasing a golf club's swing weight by wrapping lead tape around the butt of the shaft
- Counterbalancing should be avoided
- Instead of counterbalancing, adjust swing weight by adding or removing weight from the clubhead

---

Relationship Between Shaft Flexibility & Clubhead Weight

- Shaft flexibility and clubhead weight are directly related
- Adding weight to the clubhead will make the shaft perform more flexible
- Removing weight from the clubhead will make the shaft perform less flexible

Torque

Bulge

Torque

- Definition: A shaft's resistance to twisting along its longitudinal axis
- Affects the angle of the clubface at impact
- Affects how the club and ball will react at impact

Bulge

- Definition: Roundness of the clubface
- Compensates for off-center hits by moving the golf ball's center of gravity
- Example: A ball hit off the toe will start to the right of the target and hook back to the target as a result of bulge

Lie

―――――――

Loft

Lie

- Definition: Angle between the center of the golf club's shaft and a line tangent to the sole of the clubhead
- Affects the direction the clubface is pointing and how the ball leaves the clubface
- Lie angle should be fitted dynamically as the club is impacting the ball
- The shorter the club, the more upright the lie angle will be
- The longer the club, the flatter the lie angle will be
- If the lie angle is too upright, the ball will travel to the left off the clubface
- If the lie angle is too flat, the ball will travel to the right off the clubface

---

Loft

- Definition: Angle of the clubface relative to the centerline of the golf club's hosel
- Determines the golf ball's trajectory as it leaves the clubface
- If loft is altered, the hosel set and face progression will also be changed
- Adding loft to a golf club promotes bounce
- Reducing loft from a golf club promotes dig

Measuring the Loft of a Wood

———————

Face Angle

Measuring the Loft of a Wood

- Measured at a point half the distance of the clubface height on the centerline of the clubface
- Effective loft of a wood is determined by subtracting the number of degrees the club is open from the original loft. Or it is determined by adding the number of degrees the club is closed from the original loft.

Face Angle

- Definition: Angle of the clubface to the grounded sole line with the shaft perpendicular to the line of flight
- Influences the loft and direction a golf ball travels
- If the face angle is square at address, it may become closed at impact because as the shaft bows the face angle will close

Human Variables Influencing Clubhead Speed

Maximum Clubhead Speed

Human Variables Influencing Clubhead Speed

- Body flexibility
- Leverage
- Neuromuscular coordination
- Physical strength
- Swing technique

Maximum Clubhead Speed

Maximum clubhead speed is achieved by combining:
- Lightest overall weight
- Heaviest swing weight the golfer can reasonably assume

Golf Club Components

Sole Inversion

Golf Club Components

- Clubhead
- Grip
- Shaft
- If any single component of a golf club is altered, the playing characteristics of the remaining components will also be changed

---

Sole Inversion

- Definition: Angle of the sole of the golf club to the ground when the shaft is perpendicular to the ground and the clubface is square to the target
- 3 possible conditions are:
  - Bounce sole
  - Dig sole
  - Square sole

Golf Ball Trajectory

_____

Optimal Club Length

Golf Ball Trajectory

- Low center of gravity on the clubface will produce a high trajectory ball flight
- High center of gravity on the clubface will produce a low trajectory ball flight

---

Optimal Club Length

- Length that produces centeredness of contact
- Club length is a determining factor of clubhead speed
- Club length should be measured at the centerline of the shaft and <u>not</u> from the heel of the shaft to the end of the grip

Swing Plane

Lever System

Swing Plane

- Upright swing plane causes the ball to come off the clubface with a higher trajectory and a fade
- Flatter swing plane causes the ball to come off the clubface with a lower trajectory and a draw
- Flatter swing plane allows the golfer to stay better connected and time the swing more easily

---

Lever System

- The body is a series of connected levers
- One-lever swing is swinging the left arm without cocking the wrists
- Two-lever swing is swinging the left arm and cocking the wrists
- Third lever could be created by cupping the left wrist or bending the left elbow

Golf Ball Distance and Direction

Function of the Legs in the Golf Swing

Golf Ball Distance and Direction

- <u>Distance</u> is influenced by:
  - Angle of approach
  - Centeredness of contact
  - Clubhead speed
- <u>Direction</u> is influenced by:
  - Clubface position
  - Swing path
- Rotation is the primary motion used to generate power in the golf swing

---

Function of the Legs in the Golf Swing

- Serves as the platform for the rotating body and swinging arms
- Places the body in a position to strike the ball with the clubface traveling in the proper direction and at the correct angle
- Maintains body balance throughout the golf swing

Gripping the Golf Club

Grip Types

Gripping the Golf Club

Fundamentals of gripping the golf club:
- Placement: Location of the hands on the grip
- Position: Amount of hand rotation on the grip
- Pressure: How hard the grip is squeezed
- Precision: Same grip must be repeated with each swing

___

Grip Types

- <u>Interlocking grip</u> is well suited for golfers with short fingers and weak grip strength
- <u>Overlapping grip</u> is well suited for golfers with large fingers and strong hands, wrists, and forearms
- <u>Ten-finger grip</u> is well suited for young golfers with small hands

Flex Point

Casting

Flex Point

- Definition: Point at which the shaft of the golf club releases stored energy at impact
- Also referred to as the "bend point" or "kick point"
- Flex point can be low, mid, or high
- Flex point and ball flight are inversely related
    - Low flex point produces a high trajectory ball flight
    - High flex point produces a low trajectory ball flight

Casting

- Definition: Prematurely releasing the wrist on the forward swing
- Causes the clubhead to arrive at the ball before the hands and arms

Angle of Approach

———————

Centrifugal Force

Angle of Approach

- Definition: Measure of the steepness of descent of the clubhead's forward swing
- Influences the trajectory and distance a golf ball travels
- Steeper angle of approach creates more backspin, more lift, and less distance

---

Centrifugal Force

During the golf swing, centrifugal force has the following effects:
- Pulls the clubhead outward and downward
- Causes the arms to extend
- Makes the clubhead take a circular path

Positional Swing Concept

Flo-Swing Concept

Positional Swing Concept

- Firmer = more leverage
- Well suited for:
    - Athletic golfers
    - Kinesthetic golfers
    - Long hitters
    - Low handicap golfers
- Positional swing concept and flo-swing concept are the two basic swing classifications

---

Flo-Swing Concept

- Lighter = more centrifugal force
- Well suited for:
    - Beginners
    - Less athletic golfers
    - Short hitters
    - Visual golfers
- Flo-swing concept and positional swing concept are the two basic swing classifications

Arc Length & Arc Width

Golf Ball Flight Laws

Arc Length & Arc Width

- Arc length is how far back the golf club is swung
- Arc width is the extension of the golf club away from the body
- Arc width determines distance, speed, and centeredness of contact

---

Golf Ball Flight Laws

- Angle of approach
- Centeredness of contact
- Face
- Path
- Speed

Principle / Law / Preference

Swing Preferences

Principle / Law / Preference

- Principle has direct relation to, and influence on, a law
- Law is unchangeable under any set of conditions
- Preference must directly relate to a principle in order to be valid

---

Swing Preferences

- Preferences are the level at which golf instructors most often work
- An example of a swing preference is an inside takeaway
- There are endless possibilities of swing preferences

Pre-Swing Principles

In-Swing Principles

Pre-Swing Principles

- Aim
- Grip
- Setup

In-Swing Principles

- Arc length
- Arc width
- Connection
- Dynamic balance
- Impact
- Lever system
- Position
- Release
- Swing center
- Swing plane
- Timing

Kinesiology & Anatomy

───────────────

Ligament / Tendon / Cartilage

Kinesiology & Anatomy

- Kinesiology is the scientific study of human movement
- Anatomy is the science that studies the structure of the human body

---

Ligament / Tendon / Cartilage

- Ligament
    - Connective tissue that limits a muscle's range of motion
    - Connects bones to other bones to form a joint
- Tendon
    - Acts as an extension of the muscle
    - Connects muscle to bone
- Cartilage
    - Flexible connective tissue
    - Found in areas of the body such as the joints between bones, the rib cage, elbows, and knees

Muscle

Neuromuscular Coordination

Muscle

- Produces force and causes motion in the golf swing
- Produces power for movement in the skeletal structure
- Leg muscles maintain body balance throughout the golf swing
- Helps create and maintain posture during the golf swing

Neuromuscular Coordination

- Definition: Golfer's ability to integrate his or her senses with motor function to produce accurate and skilled movement
- Using the right muscles, at the right time, with the right force

Stretch Reflex

_____

Dynamic Balance

Stretch Reflex

- Definition: Muscle contraction in response to elasticity within the muscle
- Provides automatic regulation of skeletal muscle length
- Example: During the backswing, the shoulder turn may extend beyond the rotation of the trunk
- To gain the best response from a group of muscles, the muscles need to be stretched

---

Dynamic Balance

- Definition: Balance with movement
- Example: Transferring weight from a golfer's right side to left side during the golf swing
- Achieving dynamic balance is a key element of the proper golf swing

Timing / Tempo / Rhythm

Golf Car Revenue

Timing / Tempo / Rhythm

- Timing is the sequence of movements during the golf swing
- Tempo is the rate of movement during the golf swing
- Rhythm is the flow resulting from the proper relation of parts during the golf swing

---

Golf Car Revenue

- Golf cars are the second largest source of revenue for a golf facility behind playing fees
- Average golf car rental generates $1,900 revenue per year for a golf facility
- Average golf car rental fee is between $14 and $18 per round

Sources of Golf Car Revenue

Golf Car Revenue Calculation

Sources of Golf Car Revenue

- Rental fees
- Trade-in value
- Trail fees from private cars

Golf Car Revenue Calculation

Golf car revenue = # golf cars x # loops x $ per round

Golf Car Expenses

Golf Car Fleet Staff

Golf Car Expenses

- Acquisition costs
- Car path costs
- Operating expenses
- Storage costs

Golf Car Fleet Staff

Golf car fleet staff consists of:
- Attendant
- Fleet manager
- Fleet supervisor
- Maintenance supervisor
- Mechanic

Selecting Golf Car Make and Model

Selecting Golf Car Dealer

Selecting Golf Car Make and Model

Consider the following:
- Appearance
- Availability
- Comfort
- Performance
- Price
- Style
- Trade-in value
- Warranty

Selecting Golf Car Dealer

Consider the following:
- Delivery options
- Financing terms
- Parts and service availability
- Price
- Reputation
- Warranties

Golf Car Fleet Manager

Factors Affecting Golf Car Fleet

Golf Car Fleet Manager

Responsibilities include:
- Establishing policies and procedures
- Golf car acquisition
- Maintenance
- Repair
- Storage

Factors Affecting Golf Car Fleet

Golf car fleet is affected by:
- Path availability
- Terrain
- Weather
- Yardage

Golf Car Fleet Size

―――――――――

Golf Car Storage

Golf Car Fleet Size

- Average golf car fleet size is 57 cars per facility
- 1 golf car per 8 playing members
- 1 golf car per 800 rounds played annually
- Adequate storage space for a golf car is between 70 and 75 square feet per car

---

Golf Car Storage

Golf car storage requirements:
- Adequate space
- Available safety features (fire alarms and sprinklers)
- Location near clubhouse
- Proper ventilation

Leasing vs. Buying a Golf Car

Golf Car Leases

Leasing vs. Buying a Golf Car

- Leasing
  - Better from a cash flow perspective
  - Almost always under warranty
  - No resale value
- Buying
  - Results in more equity
  - Limited warranty
  - Some resale value

Golf Car Leases

- <u>Escalating lease</u> charges a lower cost in the first year of the lease and increases each year
- <u>Full maintenance fixed rate lease</u> requires the lessee to pay the same amount each month. The lessor is responsible for providing parts and services.
- <u>Lease/purchase</u> provides an option to purchase the golf car at the end of the lease
- <u>Skip payment lease</u> does not require payments during the off-season

Golf Car Acquisition

Golf Car Fleet Record Keeping

Golf Car Acquisition

Loans and other funding to acquire golf cars may be provided by:
- Banks
- Commercial finance corporations
- PGA credit union
- Savings and loans

Golf Car Fleet Record Keeping

Golf car fleet manager should maintain records for:
- Financing
- Maintenance
- Rotation

Golf Car Fleet Maintenance Types

Golf Car Fleet Maintenance Program

Golf Car Fleet Maintenance Types

Two types of golf car maintenance:
- Preventative maintenance
- Repair

_____

Golf Car Fleet Maintenance Program

Golf car fleet maintenance program should include the following elements:
- Access to proper tools and equipment
- Adequate storage space
- Ongoing staff training
- Periodic golf car inspection
- Thorough record keeping

Rules of Golf / Definitions / Appendices

Rules of Golf: 1 through 10

Rules of Golf / Definitions / Appendices

Rules of Golf contain:
- 34 rules
- 47 definitions
- 3 appendices

Rules of Golf: 1 through 10

- Rule 1: The Game
- Rule 2: Match Play
- Rule 3: Stroke Play
- Rule 4: Clubs
- Rule 5: The Ball
- Rule 6: The Player
- Rule 7: Practice
- Rule 8: Advice; Indicating Line of Play
- Rule 9: Information as to Strokes Taken
- Rule 10: Order of Play

Rules of Golf: 11 through 20

Rules of Golf: 21 through 30

Rules of Golf: 11 through 20

- Rule 11: Teeing Ground
- Rule 12: Searching for and Identifying Ball
- Rule 13: Ball Played as It Lies
- Rule 14: Striking the Ball
- Rule 15: Substituted Ball; Wrong Ball
- Rule 16: The Putting Green
- Rule 17: The Flagstick
- Rule 18: Ball at Rest Moved
- Rule 19: Ball in Motion Deflected or Stopped
- Rule 20: Lifting, Dropping and Placing; Playing from Wrong Place

---

Rules of Golf: 21 through 30

- Rule 21: Cleaning Ball
- Rule 22: Ball Assisting or Interfering with Play
- Rule 23: Loose Impediments
- Rule 24: Obstructions
- Rule 25: Abnormal Ground Conditions, Embedded Ball and Wrong Putting Green
- Rule 26: Water Hazards (Including Lateral Water Hazards)
- Rule 27: Ball Lost or Out of Bounds; Provisional Ball
- Rule 28: Ball Unplayable
- Rule 29: Threesomes and Foursomes
- Rule 30: Three-ball, Best-Ball, and Four-Ball Match Play

Rules of Golf: 31 through 34

Appendices to the Rules of Golf

Rules of Golf: 31 through 34

- Rule 31: Four-Ball Stroke Play
- Rule 32: Bogey, Par, and Stableford Competitions
- Rule 33: The Committee
- Rule 34: Disputes and Decisions

Appendices to the Rules of Golf

- Appendix I: Local Rules; Conditions of the Competition
- Appendix II: Design of Clubs
- Appendix III: The Ball

Penalty for Rule Violation

Penalty for Ethics Violation

Penalty for Rule Violation

- Penalty in stroke play for a rule violation is 2 strokes
- Penalty in match play for a rule violation is loss of hole
- Penalties apply unless otherwise noted

Penalty for Ethics Violation

Possible penalties for a PGA ethics violation:
- Monetary fine up to $1,000
- Loss of playing privileges in sectional and national events
- Suspension or expulsion from the PGA

Original Rules of Golf

Changes to the Rules of Golf

Original Rules of Golf

- Created in 1744
- 13 rules
- Originally titled "The Articles and Laws in Playing Golf"

Changes to the Rules of Golf

- Changes may be made to the Rules of Golf every 4 years
- Changes may be made to the Decisions on the Rules of Golf every 2 years
- USGA Rules Committee meets twice per year to discuss proposed rule changes
- Rules Drafting Committee is responsible for developing the language for proposed rule changes

Golf Ball Specifications

USGA and R&A

Golf Ball Specifications

- Golf balls shall weigh a maximum of 1.62 ounces
- Golf balls shall have a maximum diameter of 1.68 inches
- Specifications agreed upon by the USGA and R&A in 1920

USGA and R&A

- United States Golf Association (USGA) was founded in 1894
- Royal and Ancient Golf Club (R&A) became the governing world authority for the Rules of Golf in 1897
- USGA and R&A have not always held the same rules at the same time

Movable vs. Immovable Obstructions

———————

"Through the Green"

Movable vs. Immovable Obstructions

- Movable obstructions
    - Moved without unreasonable effort
    - Moved without delaying play
    - Moved without damage
- Immovable obstructions
    - Takes reasonable effort to move
    - Causes delay in play to move

"Through the Green"

Defined as the whole area of the golf course except:
- Teeing area of the hole being played
- Putting green of the hole being played
- All hazards on the golf course

Loose Impediments

Loose Impediment Exclusions

Loose Impediments

Natural objects such as:
- Insects
- Stones
- Twigs
- Worms

Loose Impediment Exclusions

Loose impediments exclude items that are:
- Adhering to the ball
- Embedded
- Fixed
- Growing

Identifying Ground Under Repair

Identifying Water Hazards

Identifying Ground Under Repair

Ground under repair may be identified by:
- Orange stakes, or
- White lines

Identifying Water Hazards

Water hazards may be identified by:
- Yellow stakes, or
- Yellow lines

Water Hazard Relief Options

Lateral Water Hazard Relief Options

Water Hazard Relief Options

- Play the ball as it lies
- Play the ball as near as possible from where the ball was last played
- Drop the ball on an extended line between the flagstick and where the ball last crossed the hazard

---

Lateral Water Hazard Relief Options

- Drop the ball at a point equidistant from where the ball last crossed the hazard, no nearer to the hole
- Drop the ball two club lengths from the point where the ball last crossed the hazard, no nearer to the hole

Handicap Systems

Tournament Pairing Sheet

Handicap Systems

- <u>Blind Bogey handicap system</u> matches a competitor's net score to a randomly selected number between 70 and 90
- <u>Callaway handicap system</u> deducts a number of the worst hole scores from the combined score of the first 16 holes

---

Tournament Pairing Sheet

Tournament pairing sheet includes:
- Event format
- Handicaps
- Tournament officials

PGA of America

PGA Constitution

PGA of America

- Founded in 1916
- Mission is to promote the enjoyment and involvement of the game of golf, and to contribute to its growth by providing services to golf professionals, consumers, and the golf industry
- There are approximately 28,000 men and women PGA Professionals and PGA Apprentices

---

PGA Constitution

- Article 1: Name and Purpose
- Article 2: Membership
- Article 3: Organization
- Article 4: Meetings
- Article 5: PGA Tour

Bylaws & Regulations

Penalty for PGA Constitution Rule Violation

Bylaws & Regulations

- Bylaws outline the general philosophies, practices, and procedures of the PGA Constitution, as agreed upon by the Association
- Regulations explain the Bylaws of the PGA Constitution

Penalty for PGA Constitution Rule Violation

Possible penalties for a PGA Constitution rule violation:
- Expulsion
- Probation
- Reprimand
- Suspension

PGA Officers

PGA Board of Directors

PGA Officers

- <u>President</u> serves as the Chairman of the Board, presides at all meetings, and serves as the spokesman for the Association
- <u>Vice president</u> is responsible for managing all financial matters for the Association
- <u>Secretary</u> is responsible for managing all membership matters for the Association, and serves as the Chairperson for the Board of Control
- <u>Honorary president</u> is the immediate former PGA President

---

PGA Board of Directors

PGA Board of Directors consists of:
- President
- Vice president
- Secretary
- Honorary president
- Player director
- Director from each district
- 2 independent contractors

PGA Board of Control

Golf Facility Evaluation

PGA Board of Control

- Reviews membership matters
- Meets quarterly
- Includes the PGA Secretary and four individuals appointed by the PGA President, representing the four geographical areas of the United States
- Must be a past national director, sectional officer, or national officer to serve on the Board of Control

---

Golf Facility Evaluation

Golf facilities should be evaluated on the following criteria:
- Number of members
- Number of 18-hole rounds played
- Number of lessons
- Number of bags in storage
- Number of tournaments
- Size of golf car fleet
- Merchandise sales
- Merchandise inventory levels

PGA Recognized Golf Course

PGA Recognized Golf Range

PGA Recognized Golf Course

- 9-hole golf course must be at least 1,000 yards in length
- 18-hole golf course must be at least 1,500 yards in length
- Must have at least 14 acres of total course area, excluding the clubhouse, golf shop, and parking area

---

PGA Recognized Golf Range

- Minimum of 15 tees and 150 feet of teeing area
- Depth of at least 600 feet
- PGA Professional must be available for instruction

Director of Golf
Roles & Responsibilities

General Manager
Roles & Responsibilities

Director of Golf
Roles & Responsibilities

Directs the total golf operation including:
- Golf shop
- Golf range
- Golf car fleet
- Supervision of Head Professional

General Manager
Roles & Responsibilities

- Develops annual business plan
- Implements general policies and procedures
- Maintains organizational structure
- Oversees relationship between the facility, its patrons, employees, community, government, and industry

**Head PGA Professional
Roles & Responsibilities**

**Assistant PGA Professional
Roles & Responsibilities**

Head PGA Professional Roles & Responsibilities

Head PGA Professional is responsible for:
- Handicapping
- Hiring
- Recruiting
- Starting & tee times
- Supervising
- Training

Assistant PGA Professional Roles & Responsibilities

- Bookkeeping
- Club repair
- Golf car operations
- Handicapping
- Merchandising
- Tournament operations
- Staff scheduling

PGA Apprentice Requirements

PGA Districts & Sections

PGA Apprentice Requirements

- At least 18 years old
- Eligibly employed for at least 6 months
- Endorsed by a PGA member
- High school diploma or equivalency
- Pass the Playing Ability Test (PAT)
- Pay required fees

PGA Districts & Sections

- 14 PGA Districts
- 41 PGA Sections
- In order to become a PGA Section, there must be at least 50 PGA Professionals within a 140 mile radius

Rights of PGA Members

Maintaining PGA Membership Status

Rights of PGA Members

PGA members have the right to:
- Attend annual meetings as an observer
- Hold office
- Use the PGA name and logo
- Vote

Maintaining PGA Membership Status

- Must achieve a minimum number of professional development points (PDPs) to be earned in a 3-year period, as determined by the Board of Directors
- Members who do not meet PDP requirements will be designated as Class "F" members

PGA Teaching Triangle

Methods of Learning the Golf Swing

PGA Teaching Triangle

- Three parts of the teaching triangle are what, how, and when
    - <u>What</u> the instructor selects to teach
    - <u>How</u> the instructor communicates with students
    - <u>When</u> the instructor introduces specific elements of the golf swing

---

Methods of Learning the Golf Swing

- Verbal
- Visual
- Kinesthetic (recommended form)

A-B-C Golf Swing Model

Golf Swing Learning Model

A-B-C Golf Swing Model

- Technique used to keep golf instruction simple
- Teach the golf swing in three steps
    1. Preparing to swing
    2. Top of swing
    3. Finish of swing

Golf Swing Learning Model

Four parts of the golf swing learning model:
1. Input
2. Integration
3. Output
4. Feedback

Instructor Feedback

Improving Student Motivation

Instructor Feedback

Three functions of a golf instructor providing feedback to a student:
- Fix an error
- Provide motivation
- Serve as reinforcement

Improving Student Motivation

Techniques to improve student motivation:
- Praise
- Recognition
- Reward

Evaluating Teaching Aids

Establishing Teaching Goals

Evaluating Teaching Aids

- Is the teaching aid helpful?
- Is it cost effective?
- Is it easy to set up?
- Is it easy to use?
- Is it reliable?
- Is it well made?

Establishing Teaching Goals

- Instructor and student should establish goals together
- Goals should be challenging but attainable
- Goals should be specific
- Goals should progress from short-term to long-term

Critical Error & Master Key

Teaching Drills

Critical Error & Master Key

- "Critical error" is a single error the student makes that causes additional errors to be made
- The "master key" is to fix the critical error because it will help fix other errors as well

---

Teaching Drills

Teaching drills provide the following benefits:
- Cure specific swing errors
- Isolate parts of the swing
- Promote feel
- Reinforce positive habits
- Teach correct swing position

Elements of an Employment Contract

Employment Contract Clauses

Elements of an Employment Contract

- Compensation
- Duties and responsibilities of the employer
- Duties and responsibilities of the position
- Policies on time off
- Termination clause
- Term of the contract

Employment Contract Clauses

- <u>Arbitration clause</u> specifies that any controversy or claim arising from the contract will be subject to arbitration
- <u>Evergreen clause</u> provides an automatic annual extension of the employment contract if neither party notifies the other that they wish to terminate the agreement
- <u>Inflation adjustment provision</u> provides an annual cost of living increase correlated with the Consumer Price Index
- <u>Merger clause</u> explains what will happen to a golf professional if his or her golf facility is bought or merged with another
- <u>Non-compete clause</u> specifies that an employee may not work at a competing facility for a specified period of time following separation from service

Arbitration

Deferred Compensation

Arbitration

- May be voluntary or mandatory
- May be binding or non-binding
- Less expensive than litigation
- Less time consuming than litigation
- Employment contract may specify that any controversy or claim arising from the contract will be subject to arbitration

---

Deferred Compensation

- Definition: Arrangement in which a portion of a golf professional's income is paid out at a date after which the income is actually earned
- Examples:
    - Pensions
    - Retirement plans
    - Stock options

COBRA

Fringe Benefits

COBRA

- Consolidated Omnibus Budget Reconciliation Act (COBRA)
- Employers must provide former employees and their families with the opportunity to purchase heath care coverage that is identical to the coverage they received when they were employed
- Applies to employers with 20 or more employees
- Coverage is limited to 18 months for employees
- Coverage is limited to 36 months for dependents

Fringe Benefits

Fringe benefits provided to a golf professional may include:
- Health insurance
- Life insurance
- On-duty meals
- Personal use of golf facility
- Retirement plan
- Vacation time

Child Labor Rules

Federal Employment Laws

Child Labor Rules

- 14- and 15-year-old minors may work no more than 3 hours on a school day, and 8 hours on a non-school day
- 14- and 15-year-old minors may work no more than 18 hours per week when school is in session, and 40 hours per week when school is not in session
- 14- and 15-year-old minors may not work before 7:00 am or after 7:00 pm

---

Federal Employment Laws

- <u>Age Discrimination in Employment Act (ADEA)</u> prohibits employers from discriminating against workers older than age 40
- <u>Americans with Disabilities Act (ADA)</u> prohibits employers from discriminating against a qualified disabled worker if the worker is able to perform all of the duties required for the job
- <u>Civil Rights Act of 1964</u> states that it is illegal for a company to not hire an applicant because of the applicant's gender, race, or religion

Federal Employment Laws

Federal Employment Laws

Federal Employment Laws

- Equal Pay Act of 1963 requires equal pay for equal work, regardless of sex
- Fair Credit Reporting Act requires an employer to inform the applicant in writing if they plan to conduct a background check
- Fair Labor Standards Act of 1938 set standards for minimum wage, overtime pay, child labor, and record keeping
- Garnishment Laws require a court order to have an employer withhold money from an employee's wage for payment of a debt to a third party. Applies to child support, bankruptcy, and unpaid taxes.

Federal Employment Laws

- Immigration Reform and Control Act (IRCA) requires employers to verify the identity and work status of each new employee the company hires
- Occupational Safety and Health Act (OSHA) requires employers to provide employees with a safe and healthy work environment
- Veterans Rights and Military Service Act requires companies to rehire employees who were called to, or volunteered for, military service

PGA Employment Services

Preparing for a Job Interview

PGA Employment Services

- Career Net
- Career Links
- Career Chips

Preparing for a Job Interview

- Research the facility
- Research the interviewer
- Review the facility's annual report
- Review the facility's brochure
- Provide a cover letter and résumé to each interviewer

Types of Résumés

Include / Exclude From Résumé

Types of Résumés

- Functional
- Targeted
- Chronological (most common)

Include / Exclude From Résumé

- Include on résumé:
    - Community service
    - Educational experience
    - Extracurricular activities
    - Military service
    - Objective
    - Professional affiliations
- Exclude on résumé:
    - Religious affiliations
    - Social affiliations

Networking Etiquette

Networking Etiquette

- Introduce yourself
- Request information about the golf facility
- Ask for names of decision makers
- Thank others for their time

_____

LEVEL 2

Golf Facility Mission Statement

―――――――――

SWOT Analysis

Golf Facility Mission Statement

- Guides and motivates employees
- Keeps management focused
- Includes goals regarding a golf facility's:
  - Image
  - Profitability
  - Quality of service

SWOT Analysis

- Definition: Strategic business planning tool used to evaluate a company's strengths, weaknesses, opportunities, and threats
- Strengths and weaknesses evaluate internal factors
- Opportunities and threats evaluate external factors

Golf Facility Items to Forecast

Performance Formulas

Golf Facility Items to Forecast

- Cost of goods sold
- Expenses
- Gross margin
- Number of rounds played
- Profit
- Revenue

_____

Performance Formulas

- COGS % = cost of goods sold / total retail sales
- Gross margin % = (revenue − cost of goods sold) / revenue
- Net total value = original cost − accumulated depreciation
- Profit = revenue − (cost of goods sold + expenses)

Internal Factors Affecting Economic Forecast

External Factors Affecting Economic Forecast

Internal Factors Affecting Economic Forecast

- Customer service
- Facility characteristics
- Financial resources
- Staff resources

External Factors Affecting Economic Forecast

- Golf industry trends
- National economic trends
- Regulatory trends
- Weather

Performance Analysis

Linear Trend Analysis

Performance Analysis

Two types of performance analysis:
- Linear trend analysis
- Base-year analysis

Linear Trend Analysis

- Formula: (later year sales – previous year sales) / previous year sales = % change
- Used to calculate the percentage change from year to year for line items such as number of rounds played, revenue, and expenses
- Use when there is over 5 years of historical data to compare, and the data is being compared horizontally

Base-Year Analysis

Depreciation / Amortization / Depletion

Base-Year Analysis

- Formula: (year's sales you want to compare / base year sales) x 100 = % change from base year
- Use if Head Professional wants to track improved golf shop sales relative to the year he was hired

---

Depreciation / Amortization / Depletion

- <u>Depreciation</u> is the process by which the tax basis of a tangible asset is recovered
- <u>Amortization</u> is the process by which the tax basis of an intangible asset is recovered
- <u>Depletion</u> is the process by which the tax basis of natural resources is recovered

Budgeting Process

―――――――――

Types of Budgets

Budgeting Process

1. Estimate all income and sources of income
2. Review all fixed and discretionary expenses
3. Determine how much will be saved or invested

_____

Types of Budgets

- <u>Capital budget</u> includes the cost of financing long-term projects, such as renovations to a golf course and its buildings
- <u>Cash flow budget</u> projects how much cash a golf facility will have in its bank account at the end of the budget period
- <u>Operational budget</u> provides an overview of a golf facility's day-to-day income and expenses

Elements of Effective Staffing

Policies & Procedures

Elements of Effective Staffing

- Determine staff needs
- Determine staff skills
- Establish performance standards
- Use organizational charts to establish reporting relationships

---

Policies & Procedures

- Policies are rules or principles provided by management that outline a specific course of action
- Procedures are step-by-step instructions which must be executed in a specific manner to complete a task

Procedure Writing Guidelines

Customer Service

Procedure Writing Guidelines

- Use clear and concise language
- Use simple, short words and sentences
- Start each sentence with a verb
- Provide examples
- Number each step

Customer Service

Key elements to successful customer service:
- Resources
- Staffing
- Systems

Understanding Customer Needs

"Moment of Truth"

Understanding Customer Needs

To understand customer needs, the golf professional should:
- Conduct a survey
- Host a focus group
- Review the complaint log
- Evaluate returned merchandise
- Ask customers directly

"Moment of Truth"

- Definition: Any experience customers have with a business that provides them with an opportunity to evaluate the quality of their products and services
- Example: When guests arrive at a golf club to find dirty towels lying in the locker room they are experiencing a "moment of truth"

Dissatisfied Customers

Task-Relationship Connection

Dissatisfied Customers

- 1 unhappy customer will tell 9 others
- 13% of dissatisfied customers will tell at least 20 people
- 90% of dissatisfied customers will not return to a golf facility
- 96% of dissatisfied customers will not complain directly

Task-Relationship Connection

- <u>Task</u> component
    - Identifies what the golf professional is trying to achieve
    - Golf professional should ask himself: "How does the way I handle this task build or detract from the relationship?"
- <u>Relationship</u> component
    - Identifies the quality of the interaction between the golf professional and the customer
    - Golf professional should ask himself: "How does the way I handle the relationship with the customer support or limit completing the task?"

GEODE Model

GEODE Model Examples

GEODE Model

GEODE model for handling day-to-day customer relations:
- Greet
- Enquire
- Offer
- Deliver
- Evaluate

GEODE Model Examples

- <u>Greet</u>: Golf professional frames the customer interaction as problem-solving rather than confrontational
- <u>Enquire</u>: Golf professional shows understanding and empathy, and confirms the customer's needs by restating the customer's concerns and checking for agreement
- <u>Offer</u>: Golf professional proposes a solution and describes its limitations
- <u>Deliver</u>: Golf professional determines specific arrangements and provides a meaningful extra touch
- <u>Evaluate</u>: Golf professional asks the customer for feedback

Interpersonal Skills

Interpersonal Skill Examples

Interpersonal Skills

- Act with integrity
- Encourage open expression
- Invite and give specific feedback
- Provide a compelling rationale
- Reframe difficult situations
- Show understanding
- State your purpose clearly

Interpersonal Skill Examples

- <u>Acting with integrity</u> demonstrates dependability and trustworthiness
- <u>Encouraging open expression</u> evokes participation through active involvement
- <u>Inviting and giving specific feedback</u> provides opportunity to clarify misunderstandings and change behavior
- <u>Providing a compelling rationale</u> bridges gap between what golf professional offers and what customer wants
- <u>Reframing difficult situations</u> finds positive intent that may be hidden in a negative response
- <u>Showing understanding</u> reduces defensiveness by establishing empathy
- <u>Stating your purpose clearly</u> establishes direction and alignment

Interaction Strategies

Interaction Strategy Examples

Interaction Strategies

- Convincing strategy
- Directing strategy
- Involving strategy
- Supporting strategy

Interaction Strategy Examples

- <u>Convincing</u> helps others see the value of adopting your solution
- <u>Directing</u> involves telling others explicitly what to do
- <u>Involving</u> invites others to join with your solution
- <u>Supporting</u> helps others find their own unique problem solving solution

When to Use Interaction Strategies

Golf Instructor Traits

When to Use Interaction Strategies

- <u>Convincing strategy</u> should be used by a manager if an employee is resistant and inexperienced
- <u>Directing strategy</u> should be used by a manager if an employee is enthusiastic and inexperienced
- <u>Involving strategy</u> should be used by a manager if an employee is resistant and experienced
- <u>Supporting strategy</u> should be used by a manager if an employee is enthusiastic and experienced

---

Golf Instructor Traits

Factors that make an exceptional golf instructor include:
- Communication skills
- Credibility
- Energy
- Enthusiasm
- Golf knowledge
- Motivation

Maximum Number of Lessons per Day

Methods of Acquiring Golf Knowledge

Maximum Number of Lessons per Day

- Varies according to a golf instructor's physical strength and mental stamina
- Suggested maximum number of lessons per day:
  - 10 half-hour lessons, or
  - 6 one-hour lessons

Methods of Acquiring Golf Knowledge

- Books
- Clinics
- Demonstrations
- Lessons
- Observing successful players
- Personal playing
- Seminars
- Studying videotape

Club Fitting Steps

Golf Club Evaluation

Club Fitting Steps

4. Interview the golfer regarding his swing tendencies and physical limitations
5. Evaluate the golfer's current clubs
6. Observe the golfer hitting balls
7. Provide club fitting recommendation

Golf Club Evaluation

Three elements to evaluate whether a golf club will improve a player's performance:
- Design
- Fit
- Quality

Steel Shafts

Graphite Shafts

Steel Shafts

- Flex characteristics are controlled by wall thickness
- Thinner steel shaft
    - Lighter
    - More flexible
    - More torque
- Thicker steel shaft
    - Heavier
    - Stiffer
    - Less torque

Graphite Shafts

- Transmit fewer vibrations up the shaft to golfer's hands than steel shafts
- Stiffness, flex points, and torque are controlled by:
    - Amount of fiber
    - Fiber's tensile strength
    - Pattern in which the fibers are applied

Conforming Golf Ball

Factors Affecting Golf Ball Distance

Conforming Golf Ball

Conforming golf balls must pass a test on:
- Initial velocity
- Overall distance
- Size
- Symmetry of design pattern
- Weight

Factors Affecting Golf Ball Distance

- Dimple design
- Material of the cover and core
- Size
- Weight

Factors Affecting Golf Ball Performance

Centeredness of Contact

Factors Affecting Golf Ball Performance

- Aerodynamics
- Compression
- Durability
- Material

Centeredness of Contact

Centeredness of contact is influenced by:
- Clubhead path
- Clubhead speed
- Clubface angle
- Clubface impact location

Fundamentals of Hitting an Iron Shot

Superintendent
Roles & Responsibilities

Fundamentals of Hitting an Iron Shot

- Clubhead should strike the ball with a descending arc
- Clubhead's center of gravity at impact should be equal to, or lower than, the golf ball's center of gravity

---

Superintendent
Roles & Responsibilities

- Responsible for managing the golf course, grounds surrounding the golf course, practice putting greens, golf range, parking area, and entrance road
- Hires, trains, evaluates, and manages the year-round and seasonal maintenance staff
- Oversees the turfgrass management program
- Achieves compliance with the EPA (Environmental Protection Agency) and OSHA (Occupational Safety and Health Administration)

Essential Nutrients for Turfgrass Survival

Zones of Turfgrass Adaptation

Essential Nutrients for Turfgrass Survival

- 15 essential nutrients for turfgrass survival occur naturally in sufficient quantities in the air
- 3 essential nutrients may be supplemented through fertilizers
  - Nitrogen
  - Phosphorus
  - Potassium

Zones of Turfgrass Adaptation

- Cool season grass
- Warm season grass
- Transition zone

Characteristics of Cool Season Grass

Characteristics of Warm Season Grass

Characteristics of Cool Season Grass

- Thrive in temperatures between 60 and 75 degrees
- Grass stays green all year in areas with mild winters
- Grass becomes dormant and turns brown in areas that receive snow

---

Characteristics of Warm Season Grass

- Thrive in temperatures between 80 and 95 degrees
- Grass becomes dormant and turns brown if the temperature drops below 50 degrees
- Overseeding may be used to maintain green grass all year

Northern Climate Grass

———————

Southern Climate Grass

Northern Climate Grass

- Bentgrass
- Bluegrass
- Fescue
- Ryegrass

Southern Climate Grass

- Bermudagrass
- Buffalograss
- Zoysiagrass

Function of a Plant's Roots and Shoots

Removing a Plant's Shoot

Function of a Plant's Roots and Shoots

- Roots
    - Absorb water and nutrients for the plan
- Shoots
    - Need sunlight to produce food for the plant
    - Grasses are able to regenerate their shoots if they're not cut too closely to their growing points
    - In plants, the growing point is at the tip of the shoot
    - In grass, the growing point is at the base of the shoot

---

Removing a Plant's Shoot

- Reduces a plant's resistance to the invasion of disease
- Reduces a plant's ability to absorb water and nutrients
- Reduces a plant's ability to make its own food

Types of Soil

Soil Content

Types of Soil

- Soil is classified by the size of its particles
- <u>Sandy soil</u> is composed of large particles that allow water and nutrients to pass through so quickly that they're not readily available for the plant
- <u>Clay soil</u> tends to retain water and leaves little room for oxygen
- <u>Loam soil</u> creates a stable growing environment for the plant by providing a balance between drainage and retention

---

Soil Content

Soil is approximately:
- 25% air
- 25% water
- 50% solid

Soil pH

Soil Compaction

Soil pH

- Soil pH measures soil acidity and alkalinity
- A measure of 0 is highly acidic, and a measure of 14 is highly alkaline
- Turfgrass grows best in soil that is slightly acidic (pH of 6.0 to 6.5)
- Clay soil tends to be acidic
- Sandy soil tends to be alkaline
- Lime may be added to soil to raise its pH level
- Sulfur may be added to soil to lower its pH level

Soil Compaction

- Occurs when the weight of heavy machinery compresses soil and causes a loss of pore space
- May also occur due to lack of water in the soil

Fertilizer

Syringing

Fertilizer

Bag of fertilizer that reads 10-6-4 contains:
- 10% nitrogen
- 6% phosphorus
- 4% potassium

Syringing

- Definition: Technique used to cool turfgrass through a light application of water to the grass surface
- Should be applied at the first sign of wilt
- During periods of excessive heat, syringing may be applied up to 3 times daily

Aeration

Topdressing

Aeration

- Definition: Removing 3 to 4 inches of ground soil to restore the passageways that facilitate the flow of water, nutrients, and air to the plant
- Stimulates the growth of new roots by increasing air supply to the roots
- Allows water and nutrients to penetrate into the root zone

Topdressing

- Definition: Placing a layer of soil over the putting surface to smooth and decrease surface irregularities
- Performed immediately after aerating
- Slowly alters soil content over time

Overseeding

Mowing

Overseeding

- Definition: Planting cool season grass over warm season grass
- Provides green playing surface during winter months
- Primarily used in southern areas of the country

Mowing

- Longer grass tends to be healthier than shorter grass
- Shorter heights are stressful for all types of grass
- Grasses that best tolerate shorter mowing heights are bermudagrass and bentgrass
- Shorter mowing heights create a turfgrass environment that requires more active maintenance

Mowing Heights

Mowing Frequency

Mowing Heights

- Suggested mowing height for greens is 1/8" to 1/4"
- Suggested mowing height for tees is 3/8" to 1"
- Suggested mowing height for fairways is 1/2" to 1¼"
- Suggested mowing height for rough is 2" or higher

Mowing Frequency

- Greens can be mowed once or twice per day depending on golf course conditions
- Tees and fairways should be mowed 2 to 4 times per week depending on golf course conditions
- Rough should be mowed weekly, monthly, or seasonally

Pest Categories

Pest Control

Pest Categories

Three broad categories of pests found on a golf course:
- Diseases
- Insects
- Weeds

_____

Pest Control

- Apply fungicide to eliminate diseases
- Apply herbicide to eliminate weeds
- Apply insecticide to eliminate insects

Integrated Pest Management (IPM)

Insect Prevention

Integrated Pest Management (IPM)

- Places an emphasis on pest prevention rather than eradication
- Superintendent should take appropriate but minimum action at first
- Superintendent should only take additional action if necessary to eradicate pests

_____

Insect Prevention

- Apply adequate fertilizer
- Keep thatch at a minimum
- Keep turfgrass free of weeds
- Use insecticide at first sign of insects

Surface Insects

Subsurface Insects

Surface Insects

- Surface insects found on a golf course:
  - Armyworms
  - Beetles
  - Chinch bugs
  - Cutworms
  - Fruit flies
  - Sod webworms
  - Vegetable weevils
- Turf that is beginning to die along curbs or sidewalks, even with adequate watering, is an indication that surface insects may be present

---

Subsurface Insects

- Subsurface insects found on a golf course:
  - Bermuda grass mites
  - Billbug grubs
  - Centipedes
  - Mole crickets
  - Nematodes
  - White grubs
- Overall thinning of turf is a warning sign that subsurface insects may be present

Thatch

Turfgrass Disease

Thatch

- Definition: Layer of organic matter that accumulates just below the grass blades and above the soil surface
- Thick thatch may be harmful and should be removed (dethatched)
- Excess thatch prevents water, nutrients, fertilizers, and insecticides from penetrating into the soil and plant roots

---

Turfgrass Disease

- Turfgrass disease is primarily a result of fungus
- Use fungicide at the first sign of turfgrass disease
- Turfgrass diseases include:
    - Brown patch
    - Dollar spot
    - Fairy ring
    - Grease spot (Pythium blight)

Plants & Weeds

Phases of Golf Course Design

Plants & Weeds

- Plants are classified by their lifecycle and plant structure
- A weed is defined as a plant in an undesired location
- Use herbicide to kill unwanted plants on a golf course
- Weeds grow due to soil compaction, poor drainage, excess watering, weak turfgrass, and short mowing heights

---

Phases of Golf Course Design

- Phase I: Site analysis
- Phase II: Design
- Phase III: Development
- Phase IV: Grow-in
- Phase V: Maintenance

Golf Course Design Schedule

Golf Course Design Core Team

Golf Course Design Schedule

- Phase I (site analysis) takes 4 to 6 months to complete
- Phase II (design takes 6 to 18 months to complete
- Phase III (development) takes 12 to 18 months to complete
- Phase IV (grow-in) takes 3 to 10 months to complete
- Phase V (maintenance) is ongoing and never complete

Golf Course Design Core Team

- Architect
- Contractor
- Superintendent

Phase I: Site Analysis

Hired During Phase I: Site Analysis

Phase I: Site Analysis

Golf course design core team should evaluate and review the following:
- Available resources
- Available utilities
- Compatibility
- Environmental conditions
- Land
- Legal requirements
- Political landscape

Hired During Phase I: Site Analysis

- Archaeologists
- Environmentalists
- Financial advisors
- Hydrologists
- Land planners
- Legal counsel

Phase II: Design

Hired During Phase II: Design

Phase II: Design

Design phase is completed in the following order:
1. Create base map
2. Create routing plan
3. Create concept plan
4. Create construction plan

Hired During Phase II: Design

- Building architects
- Interior designers
- Landscape architects
- Publicists

Base Map

———————

Routing Plan

Base Map

- Part of the design phase (Phase II)
- Base map includes:
  - Environmental resources
  - Historical sites
  - Right-of-ways
  - Structures
  - Underground utilities

Routing Plan

- Part of the design phase (Phase II)
- Also referred to as a schematic
- Steps to develop a routing plan:
  1. Identify possible locations for the clubhouse
  2. Identify a practice facility site at each potential clubhouse location

Concept Plan

Construction Plan

Concept Plan

- Part of the design phase (Phase II)
- Provides a visual image of how the golf course will look once it is complete
- Displays the shape, size, and form of each golf course feature, including tees, greens, bunkers, and hazards

---

Construction Plan

- Part of the design phase (Phase II)
- Guides the building of a golf course
- Includes specific plans for:
    - Grading
    - Irrigation
    - Landscaping
- Finishing the construction plan marks the end of the golf course design phase (Phase II), and the beginning of the development phase (Phase III)

Phase III: Development

Hired During Phase III: Development

Phase III: Development

Development phase is completed in the following order:
1. Staking
2. Clearing
3. Rough grading and major drainage
4. Feature construction and minor drainage
5. Irrigation
6. Finished grading and planting preparation
7. Planting

Hired During Phase III: Development

- Bricklayers
- Concrete pourers
- Heavy equipment operators
- Irrigation specialists

Phase IV: Grow-In

Irrigation System

Phase IV: Grow-In

Install and build the following:
- Chemical storage facility
- Golf car paths
- Golf car storage area
- Parking area
- Shelters
- Signs, tee markers, and ball washers

Irrigation System

Golf course irrigation system may be:
- Automatic or manual
- Single line or double line
- Electrical or hydraulic

Surface Drainage

Subsurface Drainage

Surface Drainage

- Primarily a function of the land's topography
- Determined by the slope and shape of the land

Subsurface Drainage

- Definition: Internal drainage of the soil
- Primarily a function of soil content
- Subsurface drainage may be created by:
  - Constructing drainage systems
  - Soil amendments
- Typically used in areas of the golf course that require the highest level of maintenance, such as tees and greens

Modern Methods of Greens Construction

Green Design

Modern Methods of Greens Construction

- California Greens Construction Method
- Topsoil Greens Construction Method
- USGA Greens Construction Method

_____

Green Design

- Greens typically range from 5,000 to 8,000 square feet at PGA recognized golf courses
- There should be a 12 to 15 foot collar around the perimeter of each green where no cups should be placed
- Each green should have 12 to 20 areas for possible cup placement, with a 3 foot radius around each cup with no slope
- Greens should vary in size, shape, and contour
- Greens should hold a well-played approach shot

Tee Area Design

Use of Hazards on a Golf Course

Tee Area Design

- Tee area for each hole should be at least 6,000 square feet
- Because they receive more wear, the first, tenth, and par-3 tees typically average 8,000 square feet or more
- Golfers should be able to view the entire hole from the tee area
- Contour of the tee area should direct golfers towards the intended line of play

---

Use of Hazards on a Golf Course

- Integrate natural features when possible
- Hazards are intended to:
    - Challenge golfers
    - Direct play
    - Provide depth perception
    - Provide variety

Golf Course Design
Safety Considerations

Routing a Golf Course

Golf Course Design Safety Considerations

- Adjacent tees and greens should be at least 100 feet apart at their borders
- Adjacent tees and greens should be at least 200 feet apart from their center points
- If space limitations require holes to be located close together, use bunkers, ponds, mounds, and trees to separate the holes

---

Routing a Golf Course

- Golf holes should be routed clockwise
- Allow right-handed golfers to slice into the course, not out of bounds

Managing Golf Course Traffic

Planting a Newly Designed Golf Course

Managing Golf Course Traffic

- Allow golf cars only in designated areas
- Limit play
- Post signs, course markers, and barriers
- Rotate cup placement on greens
- Rotate tee markers

Planting a Newly Designed Golf Course

Plant in the following order:
1. Tees and greens
2. Fairways
3. Rough

Types of Golf Holes

Golf Course Renovation

Types of Golf Holes

- <u>Heroic golf holes</u> require extraordinary maneuvers
- <u>Penal golf holes</u> are not forgiving because they leave little room for error
- <u>Strategic golf holes</u> require thought and consideration

---

Golf Course Renovation

Reasons to renovate a golf course:
- Change in golf technology
- Change in market demand
- Environmental evolution

Recreational Golf Experience Phases

Recreational Golf Experience Phases

1. Anticipation
2. Arrival
3. Participation
4. Cool down
5. Memory

LEVEL 3

Merchandising Steps

Open-to-Buy (OTB) Plan

Merchandising Steps

1. Create open-to-buy (OTB) plan
2. Create merchandise assortment plan (MAP)
3. Select vendor
4. Determine price
5. Order and receive merchandise
6. Display and promote merchandise
7. Sell merchandise
8. Monitor sales and inventory levels
9. Make adjustments as needed

Open-to-Buy (OTB) Plan

- Helps a golf professional determine how much money should be spent on merchandise classifications
- Tracks how much money will remain each month to buy or restock inventory
- Maintains inventory levels to support expected future sales
- In an OTB plan, approximately 10% to 25% of all dollars should be uncommitted to allow for flexibility and periodic changes in purchasing

Establishing an Open-to-Buy (OTB) Plan

Merchandise Classifications

Establishing an Open-to-Buy (OTB) Plan

1. Forecast sales
2. Forecast cost of goods sold
3. Forecast turnover rate
4. Establish beginning-of-month inventory levels
5. Calculate OTB plan budget

Merchandise Classifications

- Examples include men's apparel, women's apparel, shoes, gloves, etc.
- Small golf shops typically have at least 10 merchandise classifications
- Large golf shops have 20 or more merchandise classifications

Cost of Goods Sold (COGS)

Cost of Goods Sold as a Percentage of Sales

Cost of Goods Sold (COGS)

- Definition: Wholesale price vendors charge for merchandise
- Includes additional costs such as shipping and handling
- Includes merchandise that has been lost or stolen
- COGS $ = beginning of month inventory + purchases – end of month inventory
- COGS % = cost of goods sold in dollars / total retail sales

_____

Cost of Goods Sold as a Percentage of Sales

- Should be between 65% and 75% for hard goods
- Should be between 50% and 60% for soft goods
- "Soft goods" are defined as products consumed in one use

Inventory Turnover Rate

Average Turnover Rate Comparison

Inventory Turnover Rate

- Definition: Indicates how many times a golf shop's average inventory is sold and reinvested throughout the year
- Turnover rate = total cost of goods sold / average inventory at cost
- The higher a golf shop's inventory turnover rate, the less inventory is needed on hand to reach sales goals
- Highest turnover items are golf balls and shirts
- Excessively high turnover can lead to a higher cost of goods sold percentage
- Poor pricing will result in poor turnover

Average Turnover Rate Comparison

- Average turnover rate for all golf shops is 1.5
- Average turnover rate for private equity PGA facilities is 2.5
- Average turnover rate for all sporting retailers is 3.6
- Average turnover rate for top golf merchandisers is 4.0

Inventory Levels

Inventory Tracking Systems

Inventory Levels

- Average monthly inventory level = annual COGS / turnover rate
- Average inventory at cost = total end of month inventory on hand / length of season
- Inventory levels should increase two months before the peak season begins
- Enough inventory should be on hand at the beginning of the season to cover sales for at least 90 days
- Physical inventory count should be performed at least twice per year

---

Inventory Tracking Systems

- <u>Financial value inventory tracking</u> indicates the dollar value of inventory on hand and sold, and the history of price changes and markdowns
- <u>Perpetual book inventory tracking</u> indicates changes to merchandise levels, both in terms of dollar value and number of units, on a daily basis or as they occur
- <u>Physical unit inventory tracking</u> indicates the quantity of merchandise on hand, sold, and on order, and the age of the merchandise

Merchandise Assortment Plan (MAP)

Establishing a Merchandise Assortment Plan (MAP)

Merchandise Assortment Plan (MAP)

- Establishes the sizes, colors, materials, models, styles, brands, price points, and quantities for each product line
- Merchandise should be selected on the basis of:
  - Brand name
  - Compatibility
  - Competition
  - Customer demand
  - Profitability
  - Supply

Establishing a Merchandise Assortment Plan (MAP)

1. Review customer needs
2. Evaluate the previous year's performance by merchandise classification
3. Research market trends
4. Select merchandise to purchase

Vendor Selection

Vendor Concentration

Vendor Selection

Vendors should be selected on the basis of:
- Advertising support
- Assistance with backroom operations (pricing and tagging)
- Extended billing options
- Product discounts

Vendor Concentration

- Concentrating a golf shop's buying power with few vendors has advantages and disadvantages
- Advantages
    - Faster delivery
    - Individual attention
    - Improved efficiency
    - Quantity discounts
- Disadvantages
    - Fewer sources of information
    - Less access to new trends
    - Possible stock outages

Planogram

Extended Billing Strategies

Planogram

- Definition: Golf shop floor plan that illustrates where different types of merchandise should be placed
- Departmentalizing a golf shop is part of an effective planogram
- Group merchandise by vendor, size, color, etc.
- Establish "destination areas" in the golf shop that include products customers intend to purchase before entering the shop

---

Extended Billing Strategies

- Types of extended billing strategies include anticipation dating and spring dating
- Anticipation dating
  - Setting a future date when payment is due
  - Offering a discount for early payment
- Spring dating
  - Golf shop receives merchandise in the fall of the current year, with payment due in April or May of the following year
- Advantages of using extended billing strategies include the opportunity to sell items at no immediate cost, and a reduced number of back orders

Product Markup Approaches

Product Markup Examples

Product Markup Approaches

- Cost plus markup
- Keystoning
- Manufacturer's suggested retail price
- Mill River Plan

Product Markup Examples

- <u>Cost plus markup</u>: Use a target markup percentage as the basis for pricing merchandise
- <u>Keystoning</u>: Double an item's cost to arrive at the final retail price
- <u>Manufacturer's suggested retail price</u>: Golf shop sets prices according to the manufacturer's suggested retail price
- <u>Mill River Plan</u>: Members pay an initial fee at the beginning of the season and can purchase merchandise at a small percentage above cost

Markup & Margin Formulas

Determining Product Markup

Markup & Margin Formulas

- Markup $ = retail price – cost
- Markup % = markup $ / cost
- Gross margin $ = retail price – cost
- Gross margin % = markup $ / retail price

Determining Product Markup

- Establish gross margin goals first, then determine what the product markup must be in order to achieve it
- Gross profit margin for a public golf facility should be at least 30%
- Gross profit margin for a private golf facility should be at least 50%
- Actual gross margin will be less than markup because some items will be lost, stolen, or damaged

Competitive Factors Influencing Markup

Value Added Factors Influencing Markup

Competitive Factors Influencing Markup

- Exclusivity
- Follow the leader
- Opportunistic pricing
- Supply and demand

Value Added Factors Influencing Markup

- Convenience
- Facility image
- Product availability
- Services provided

Key Performance Indicators

Gross Margin Return on Investment (GMROI)

Key Performance Indicators

- COGS as a % of sales
- Gross margin $
- Gross margin %
- Gross margin return on investment (GMROI)
- Inventory turnover rate
- Revenue per round

Gross Margin Return on Investment (GMROI)

- Calculates the profit made for each dollar spent on inventory
- Measures the true profitability of different products, such as those that have high margins (golf shoes) and those that have high turnover (golf tees)
- Golf shop GMROI between 110% and 160% is excellent
- GMROI = gross margin in dollars / total retail sales

Merchandise Markdowns

Temporary vs. Permanent Markdowns

Merchandise Markdowns

Merchandise markdowns provide the following benefits:
- Decrease inventory levels
- Increase cash flow
- Remove stale merchandise
- Stimulate sales

Temporary vs. Permanent Markdowns

- Temporary markdown
  - Also referred to as a "point-of-sale" markdown
  - Takes place during special events
- Permanent markdown
  - Permanent reduction in a product's list price
  - Should be indicated on merchandise tags

Methods of Improving Financial Performance

Consequences of Poor Pricing

Methods of Improving Financial Performance

- Adjust prices
- Decrease inventory costs
- Increase sales volume

Consequences of Poor Pricing

- Bankruptcy or job loss
- Excess inventory
- Failure to reach financial goals
- Lost sales
- Poor turnover

Effective Pricing Strategies

Purchase Order (PO)

Effective Pricing Strategies

Effective pricing strategies provide the following benefits:
- Ability to meet overhead costs
- Ability to meet profit goals
- Consistent sales volume

———————

Purchase Order (PO)

Purchase orders identify the following:
- What merchandise is on order
- When merchandise was ordered
- When merchandise will be delivered
- Who ordered merchandise

Point-of-Sale (POS) System

Elements of an Attractive Buying Environment

Point-of-Sale (POS) System

- Allows for timely reporting of sales information
- Automatically updates a golf shop's open-to-buy (OTB) plan
- Maintains accurate inventory
- Maintains price control

Elements of an Attractive Buying Environment

- Displays
- Fixtures
- Floor layout
- Lighting
- Signage
- Staff selling skills

Displays & Fixtures

Sizing Merchandise

Displays & Fixtures

- Attention-getting displays
  - Create changing elevations
  - Highlight a coordinated look
  - Make merchandise easily accessible
- Flexible fixtures
  - Enhance the golf shop's image
  - Keep the golf shop looking full when inventory is low
  - Present older merchandise in a new light

_____

Sizing Merchandise

- Hanging merchandise
  - Size items from left to right
  - Begin with the smallest size and increase size as you move to the right
- Folded merchandise
  - Size items from top to bottom
  - Begin with the smallest size and increase size as you move to the bottom

Maintaining a Golf Shop's Appearance

Managing a Golf Shop

Maintaining a Golf Shop's Appearance

- Daily activities
    - Clean displays and mirrors
    - Organize the counter area
    - Vacuum the floor
- Weekly activities
    - Clean air vents
    - Clean shelves
    - Organize the back room

Managing a Golf Shop

Golf professional should perform the following functions:
1. Track sales performance
2. Analyze variances in sales
3. Adjust factors as needed

Preparing for a Promotional Event

Selling Process Steps

Preparing for a Promotional Event

1. Set objectives
2. Establish the budget
3. Determine requirements
4. Identify tasks to be completed
5. Schedule activities
6. Communicate the plan to employees

Selling Process Steps

1. Approach the customer
2. Collect key information
3. Present the merchandise
4. Close the sale
5. Build future sales

Delegating

Resources / Input / Feedback

Delegating

- Definition: Partnership building process that empowers employees
- <u>Not</u> a technique used to control employees
- Manager should consider the capabilities and willingness of an employee before delegating an assignment

---

Resources / Input / Feedback

- <u>Resources</u> are the basic means available to an employee in completing a task
- <u>Input</u> is the information, circumstances, or events that prompt an employee to take action to complete a task
- <u>Feedback</u> is the specific information an employee receives about the results of his or her actions

Types of Resources

Feedback Guidelines

Types of Resources

Resources can be:
- Financial
- Human
- Material
- Time-based

Feedback Guidelines

Effective feedback is:
- Based on fair expectations
- Easy to understand
- Objective
- Specific to an employee's actions
- Timely

Building Blocks of Motivating Work

Elements of an Effective Work Environment

Building Blocks of Motivating Work

Three building blocks of motivating work:
- The performer
- The work assignment
- The work environment

Elements of an Effective Work Environment

- Fair treatment by the manager
- Relevant rules
- Satisfactory work conditions
- Stable work relationship between the manager and employees

Principles of Motivating Work

4-Stage Sequence for Correcting Performance Problems

Principles of Motivating Work

- Autonomy
- Feedback
- Significant work
- Skill variety
- Whole task

4-Stage Sequence for Correcting Performance Problems

- Stage 1: Joint problem solving with performer
- Stage 2: Reinforced problem solving with performer
- Stage 3: Final decision making with performer
- Stage 4: Termination of employment relationship

Failure to Correct Performance Problems

Teaching Philosophy

Failure to Correct Performance Problems

Four ways a manager can fail to correct performance problems:
- Failure to involve the employee
- Inaction
- Missed opportunities
- Wrong assumptions

Teaching Philosophy

- Definition: A golf instructor's mission statement
- Summarizes an instructor's views, beliefs, concepts, and attitudes towards the game of golf and how it should be taught
- Instructor must be able to describe and defend each element of his teaching philosophy

Teaching Approach

Putting Principles

Teaching Approach

- How an instructor communicates with students
- Procedure for executing an instructor's teaching philosophy
- Changes with each student

Putting Principles

- Position eye line over, or slightly inside, the ball
- Square the clubface to the target
- Position the ball forward of center
- Limit body movement
- Use an accelerating stroke

Putting Grip

Putter Characteristics

Putting Grip

- Select the putting grip that will:
    o   Resist wristiness
    o   Resist clubface rotation
- Reverse overlap is most common putting grip

Putter Characteristics

- Average length is 35.5 inches
- Average lie is 73.5 degrees
- Average loft is 4.0 degrees
- Average weight is 11.5 ounces

Grain

Chipping vs. Pitching

Grain

- Bermudagrass has the most grain
- Shiny putting surface means the grain is moving away from the golfer
- Dull putting surface means the grain is moving towards the golfer
- Grain has little effect on a putt's break
- Grain has more effect on the speed of a putt

Chipping vs. Pitching

- Chipping
    - More ground time than air time for the golf ball
    - One-lever stroke (firm wrists)
    - Vertical centerline of the golfer's body should be 2 inches in front of the ball
- Pitching
    - More air time than ground time for the golf ball
    - Two-lever stroke (cocked wrists)
    - Vertical centerline of the golfer's body should be even with the ball
- Transition from chipping to pitching by moving the ball to the centerline of the golfer's body using a wedge

Principles of Chipping & Pitching

Practice Shot Routine

Principles of Chipping & Pitching

- Grip pressure should be firm or light, but never tight
- Firm grip pressure slows clubhead speed, and light grip pressure increases it
- Feet and hips should be open to restrict the backswing for greater control
- Choke down on the golf club for better control
- Move the ball back in stance if the lie is bare, or to produce a low trajectory ball flight
- Move the ball forward in stance if the lie is fluffy, or to produce a high trajectory ball flight

---

Practice Shot Routine

1. Survey the lie, terrain, and other external conditions
2. Visualize the shot you want to hit
3. Rehearse the swing until the correct feel is achieved
4. Execute the rehearsed swing
5. Evaluate the shot

Principles of Hitting a Cut Shot

Principles of Hitting a Cut-Lob Shot

Principles of Hitting a Cut Shot

To hit a cut shot:
- Aim the feet and shoulders to the left of the target
- Open the clubface
- Keep the hands and arms back
- Move the body forward

Principles of Hitting a Cut-Lob Shot

To hit a cut-lob shot:
- Move the ball forward in stance
- Open the clubface
- Swing with the arms

Principles of Hitting a Flop Shot

Principles of Hitting a Draw

Principles of Hitting a Flop Shot

To hit a flop shot:
- Allow the left wrist to break downward
- Strike the ball with a steep descent
- Maintain wristy action through the golf ball

Principles of Hitting a Draw

To hit a draw:
- Sole the clubface square to the target
- Use a closed face grip
- Aim the feet and shoulders to the right of the target

Uneven Lies

Sand Wedge Characteristics

Uneven Lies

- Sidehill lie with ball above the feet: Tendency is to chunk, pull, or hook the ball
- Sidehill lie with ball below the feet: Tendency is to push, slice, or top the ball
- Uphill lie: Tendency is to chunk, pull, or hit behind the ball
- Downhill lie: Tendency is to top, push, or hit behind the ball

---

Sand Wedge Characteristics

- To easily remove the ball from a greenside bunker, a sand wedge has:
  - Breadth
  - Camber
  - Sole inversion
- Gene Sarazan is credited with inventing the modern sand wedge

Breadth & Camber

Greenside Bunker Shot

Breadth & Camber

- Breadth is the width of a golf club's sole
- Camber is the curvature of a golf club's sole
- Camber helps irons move smoothly across the turf and dig less into the ground when taking divots

---

Greenside Bunker Shot

- Play the ball 4 to 6 inches left of the golfer's vertical centerline
- Bounce is promoted if the heel of the golf club leads
- Dig is promoted if the toe of the golf club leads
- "V" shaped swing will produce a higher, softer shot
- "U" shaped swing will produce a lower, longer shot

Controlling Distance on Bunker Shots

Buried Greenside Bunker Shot

Controlling Distance on Bunker Shots

Distance is controlled by:
- Angle of approach
- Blade position
- Length of backswing
- Length of follow through
- Pace of backswing
- Volume of sand

Buried Greenside Bunker Shot

To hit a buried greenside bunker shot:
- Play the ball back in stance to increase penetration with the clubface
- Turn the toe of clubhead in for a knife-like leading edge to easily penetrate through the sand

Fairway Bunker Shot

Wind Conditions

Fairway Bunker Shot

- Contact the ball first when hitting from a fairway bunker
- Choke down on the club as far down as the golfer's feet are buried in the sand
- Firm sand requires less bounce
- Soft sand requires more bounce

Wind Conditions

- Wind against the golfer
    - Choose a stronger club
    - Choke down on the club for better control
    - Move the ball back in stance
    - Shorten the swing
- Downwind
    - Tee the ball higher
    - Do not over swing
- Side wind
    - Let the ball ride the wind for maximum distance
    - Do not fight the wind

Body Types

Endomorph

Body Types

3 basic human body types:
- Endomorph
- Ectomorph
- Mesomorph

Endomorph

- Endomorph is characterized by:
    - Low muscle tone
    - Small bones
    - Soft, round frame
- Endomorphs are generally poor athletes

Ectomorph

Mesomorph

Ectomorph

- Ectomorph is characterized by:
    - Long arms and legs
    - Short trunk
    - Thin bones
    - Thin muscles
- Ectomorphs generally have high endurance levels

Mesomorph

- Mesomorph is characterized by:
    - Big bones
    - Broad shoulders
    - Large muscles
    - Slender waist
- Mesomorphs generally have increased strength

Senior Golfers

Group Lessons

Senior Golfers

- Need to adopt a more clockwise-positioned grip to reduce forearm and hand rotation
- Senior golfers typically experience:
  - Decreased strength
  - Decreased range of motion

Group Lessons

- <u>Semi-private teaching lesson</u> includes 2 to 4 students
- <u>Group lesson</u> should be limited to 5 to 12 students in total, allowing 3 to 5 minutes each for individual instruction

Golf Clinics

Teaching Left-Handed Golfers

Golf Clinics

- <u>Participation clinic</u> includes a blend of demonstration, observation, and coaching students while they hit golf balls
- <u>Demonstration clinic</u> educates and entertains students by blending fun with fundamentals

---

Teaching Left-Handed Golfers

- Right-handed golf instructor should use himself as a mirror image to teach swing fundamentals to a left-handed student
- Although 10% to 15% of Americans are left-handed, only 3% to 6% play golf left-handed

Factors Affecting a Golfer's Skill Level

Types of Golf Facilities

Factors Affecting a Golfer's Skill Level

- Cardiovascular endurance
- Flexibility
- Muscular endurance
- Strength

Types of Golf Facilities

- Public
- Private
- Semi-private

Types of Private Golf Facilities

Equity Golf Facility

Types of Private Golf Facilities

- Developer-owned
- Equity
- Privately managed

Equity Golf Facility

- Type of private golf facility
- Owned by the golf club's members
- Service, not profit, is the operational goal

Privately Managed Golf Facility

Food & Beverage Operation

Privately Managed Golf Facility

- Type of private golf facility
- Goals include:
    - High profit
    - Full membership

Food & Beverage Operation

- Primary goal is to achieve total customer satisfaction
- At least 50% of a golf facility's non-dues related income should come from the food and beverage operation
- Largest expense in a typical food and beverage operation is payroll, followed by supplies

Food & Beverage Inventory Control

P-A-C-E

Food & Beverage Inventory Control

- "Par stock" refers to the predetermined quantities of food items the Food and Beverage Director wants to have on hand at all times
- Food and beverage purchasing is generally based on the bid system

---

P-A-C-E

- Successful food and beverage operations follow the acronym P-A-C-E
- P-A-C-E stands for:
    - Primary plan
    - Alternative plan
    - Contingency plan
    - Emergency plan

Food Cost Control

Picture Board

Food Cost Control

- Definition: Following the golf facility's predetermined standards, while exercising restraint over the price the facility pays to purchase, prepare, and sell food
- Applies to the following areas:
  - Menu
  - Purchasing
  - Receiving
  - Service
  - Storeroom

Picture Board

- Demonstrates the standard plate presentation
- Should be maintained in the kitchen
- Maintains consistency for the food and beverage operation

Menu

Menu Development Steps

Menu

- Menu is the most basic and important control tool used in a food and beverage operation
- To determine a menu item's base selling price, multiply the entrée cost by the price multiplier
- Price multiplier is equal to 100% divided by the food cost goal
- Menu item's standard portion cost = total cost of recipe / number of portions

---

Menu Development Steps

1. Develop the menu concept
2. Develop recipes
3. Test recipes
4. Determine menu costs
5. Print the menu
6. Train staff

Standard Recipe

Elements of a Standard Recipe

Standard Recipe

- Definition: Blueprint used to develop a food and beverage menu item
- Benefits of using a standard recipe:
    - Less supervision required
    - Product consistency
    - Standard portion cost
    - Standard portion size

Elements of a Standard Recipe

- Ingredients
- Quantities
- Preparation procedure
- Portion size
- Garnish

Levels of Food & Beverage Service

Food & Beverage Staffing Levels

Levels of Food & Beverage Service

Six levels of food and beverage service in the golf industry:
- Banquets
- Carryout
- Formal fine dining
- Full service
- Off-site catering
- On-course concessions

Food & Beverage Staffing Levels

- Carryout service
    - 1 attendant per 20 to 30 rounds of golf per hour
- Formal fine dining
    - 1 cook per 10 customers
    - 1 dishwasher per 2 servers and cooks
    - 1 front server per 12 customers
    - 1 maitre d' per 4 front servers

Food & Beverage Staffing Levels

_____

Stages of the Hiring Process

Food & Beverage Staffing Levels

- Full service
    - 1 bartender / busser / host / washer per 5 to 6 servers
    - 1 cook and server per 12 customers per hour
- Off-site catering
    - 1 bartender per 100 customers
    - 1 server per 2 tables for plated meals
    - 1 server per 3 tables for a buffet
    - 1 server per 30 customers for a reception
- On-course concessions
    - 1 attendant per 50 to 60 rounds of golf

Stages of the Hiring Process

1. Recruiting
2. Interviewing
3. Hiring
4. Orientation

Staff Orientation

Methods Used to Retain Staff

Staff Orientation

- Answer employee questions
- Explain employee benefits
- Explain pay periods
- Review policies and procedures
- Tour the facility

Methods Used to Retain Staff

- Offer advancement opportunities
- Provide adequate compensation
- Provide thorough training

Characteristics of a Well-Maintained Storeroom

Dram Shop Laws

Characteristics of a Well-Maintained Storeroom

- A well-maintained storeroom has carefully regulated:
    - Air circulation
    - Humidity
    - Sanitation
    - Temperature
- A well-maintained storeroom uses the FIFO (first-in-first-out) inventory management method

---

Dram Shop Laws

- Holds liquor-serving establishments liable for the actions of their customers
- Encourages restaurant and bar operators to use sound judgment when serving liquor

Liquor Service Policies

Failing to Comply With
Food & Beverage Regulations

Liquor Service Policies

- Liquor license must be obtained before offering liquor for sale
- Liquor license must be displayed at all times
- Liquor-serving establishments must purchase liquor from a licensed vendor

---

Failing to Comply With Food & Beverage Regulations

Possible penalties for failing to comply with food and beverage regulations:
- Closing the food and beverage operation
- Lawsuit
- Loss of license, permit, or certificate
- Monetary fine

ABOUT THE AUTHORS

Ryan Brandeburg is a PGA member and serves as the Director of Golf for The Lodge at Kauri Cliffs and The Farm at Cape Kidnappers on the North Island of New Zealand. Both golf courses consistently rank among the top 50 in the world, and Ryan's responsibilities include managing the daily operations and strategic direction for each course. Ryan has an extensive background in private and resort operations, and has formerly served as the Acting Director of Golf at Waldorf Astoria Golf Club in Orlando, Florida, and the Head Golf Professional at Naples Grande Golf Club in Naples, Florida. In addition, Ryan is a contributing columnist to international golf publications including Golf Digest Korea and Golf Travel China.

Matthew Brandeburg is a Certified Financial Planner in Columbus, Ohio. He serves as the Chief Operating Officer for a fee-only financial planning firm with over $500 million in assets under management and he's an active member of the National Association of Personal Financial Advisors (NAPFA). Matthew is the author of the books "Financial Planning For Your First Job," "Your Guide to the CFP Certification Exam," and "CFP Certification Exam Practice Question Workbook." In addition, he teaches the class "Financial Planning in your 20s and 30s" at Ohio State University.

INDEX

A

A-B-C golf swing model, 103-104
Accelerating stroke, 278
Accumulated depreciation, 132
Acidic, 180
Acquisition cost, 48
Advancement opportunity, 324
Advertising, 242
Aerating/aeration, 183-184
Aerodynamics, 166
Age Discrimination in Employment Act (ADEA), 118
Aim, 36, 286, 288
Air circulation, 326
Air supply, 184
Alkaline, 180
Americans with Disabilities Act (ADA), 118
Amortization, 137-138
Anatomy, 37-38
Angle of approach, 22, 27-28, 32, 294
Annual report, 122
Anticipation dating, 244
Appendix to Rules of Golf, 66
Approach shot, 216
Arbitration, 112-114
Arc length, 31-32, 36
Arc width, 31-32, 36
Archaeologist, 202
Architect, 200, 204
Armyworms, 194
Articles and Laws in Playing Golf, 70
Assistant PGA Professional, 95-96
Athletic golfer, 30
Attendant, 48, 320, 322
Autonomy, 274
Average inventory, 236, 238

B

Back order, 244
Background check, 120
Backroom operations, 242
Backspin, 28
Backswing, 42, 284, 294

Balance, 22, 36, 40-42
Ball above feet, 290
Ball below feet, 290
Ball flight, 18, 26, 31-32, 284
Ball in motion, 64
Bank, 58, 140
Bankruptcy, 120, 256
Banquet, 320
Bar, 326
Bare lie, 284
Bartender, 322
Base map, 204-206
Base selling price, 316
Base-year analysis, 136-138
Beetles, 194
Bentgrass, 174, 186
Bermuda grass mites, 194
Bermudagrass, 174, 186, 282
Best-ball, 64
Bid system, 312
Billbug grubs, 194
Blade position, 294
Blind bogey handicap system, 82
Bluegrass, 174
Board of Control, 88-90
Body flexibility, 14, 306
Body type, 297-298
Bogey, 66
Bookkeeping, 96
Bounce, 10, 16, 292, 296
Brand, 240
Breadth, 290-292
Bricklayer, 210
Brochure, 122
Brown patch, 196
Budget, 139-140, 232, 266
Budgeting process, 139-140
Buffalograss, 174
Buffet, 322
Bulge, 7-8
Bunker, 208, 220, 290-296
Buried lie, 293-294, 296
Business plan, 94, 130
Buying environment, 259-260
Bylaws, 85-86

C

California Greens Construction Method, 216
Callaway handicap system, 82
Camber, 290-292
Car path, 48, 52, 212
Cardiovascular endurance, 306
Career Chips, 122
Career Links, 122
Career Net, 122
Cartilage, 37-38
Cash flow, 56, 140, 254

Cash flow budget, 140
Casting, 25-26
Center of gravity, 8, 18, 168
Centeredness of contact, 18, 22, 32, 165-166
Centerline, 10, 12, 18, 282, 292
Centipedes, 194
Centrifugal force, 27-28, 30
Chairman of the Board, 88
Changes to Rules of Golf, 69-70
Child labor rules, 117-118, 120
Chinch bugs, 194
Chip, 281-284
Choke down, 284, 296
Chronological resume, 124
Chunk shot, 290
Civil Rights Act of 1964, 118
Class "F" member, 100
Clay soil, 178, 180
Cleaning ball, 64
Clearing, 210
Closed clubface, 12
Closed face grip, 288
Club fitting, 10, 159-160
Club repair, 96
Clubface, 8, 10, 12, 16, 18, 20, 22, 166, 278, 280, 286, 288, 294
Clubface impact location, 166
Clubface rotation, 280
Clubhead, 4-6, 10, 13-14, 16, 18, 22, 26, 28, 166, 168, 284, 294
Clubhead path, 166
Clubhead speed, 13-14, 18, 22, 166, 168, 284
Clubhead weight, 5-6
Clubhouse, 54, 92, 206
COBRA, 115-116
Collar, 216
Committee, 66, 70
Compensation, 112-114, 324
Competition, 66, 240
Competitive factor, 249-250
Complaint log, 146
Compression, 166
Concept plan, 204, 207-208
Conforming golf ball, 163-164
Connective tissue, 38
Construction plan, 204, 207-208
Contour, 216, 218
Contractor, 88, 200
Cook, 320, 322
Cool season grass, 170-172, 186

Cost of goods sold (COGS), 132, 232-234, 236, 238, 252
Cost plus markup, 246
Counterbalancing, 4-6
Course marker, 212, 222
Cover letter, 122
Critical error, 109-110
Cup placement, 216, 222
Customer demand, 224, 240, 250
Customer needs, 145-146, 240
Customer service, 134, 143-144
Cut shot, 285-286
Cut-lob shot, 285-286
Cutworms, 194

D

Decisions on Rules of Golf, 70
Deferred compensation, 113-114
Definitions of Rules of Golf, 61-62
Delegating, 267-268
Demonstration clinic, 304
Departmentalizing, 244
Depletion, 137-138
Depreciation, 132, 137-138
Depth perception, 218
Descending arc, 168
Design, 66, 160, 164, 197-200, 202-204, 206, 208, 215-222
Design phase (Phase II), 198, 200, 203-204, 206, 208
Destination area, 244
Dethatch, 196
Developer-owned golf facility, 308
Development phase (Phase III), 198, 200, 208-210
Dig, 10, 16, 292
Dimple design, 164
Director of golf, 93-94
Disabled worker, 118
Discount, 242, 244
Discrimination, 118
Disease, 176, 190, 195-196
Dissatisfied customer, 147-148
Distance, 12, 21-22, 28, 32, 163-164, 293-294, 296
Divot, 292
Dollar spot, 196
Dormant, 172
Downhill lie, 290
Downwind, 296
Drainage, 178, 198, 210, 213-214
Drainage system, 214
Dram shop law, 325-326

Draw, 20, 287-288
Dynamic balance, 36, 41-42

E

Economic trends, 134
Ectomorph, 298-300
Effective loft, 12
18-hole golf course, 90, 92
Elasticity, 42
Elbow, 20, 38
Embedded ball, 64, 76
Employee benefits, 115-116, 324
Employment contract, 111-112, 114
Endomorph, 297-298
Endurance, 300, 306
Entrance road, 168
Entrée cost, 316
Environmental conditions, 202
Environmental evolution, 224
Environmental Protection Agency (EPA), 168
Environmental resource, 206
Environmentalist, 202
Equal Pay Act of 1963, 120
Equity golf facility, 307-308
Escalating lease, 56

Essential nutrient, 169-170
Ethics violation, 67-68
Event format, 82
Evergreen clause, 112
Expenses, 47-48, 132, 136, 140, 310
Expulsion from PGA, 68, 86
Extended billing, 242-244

F

Face angle, 12, 166
Face progression, 10
Facility characteristics, 134
Facility image, 250
Fade, 20
Fair Credit Reporting Act, 120
Fair Labor Standards Act of 1938, 120
Fairway, 188, 222
Fairway bunker, 295-296
Fairy ring, 196
Feature construction, 210
Federal employment laws, 117-120
Feedback, 104-106, 150, 152, 267-270, 274
Feel, 4, 110, 284
Fertilizer, 170, 181-182, 192, 196
Fescue, 174
Fiber, 162
FIFO (first-in-first-out), 326

Financial advisor, 202
Financial performance, 131-132, 135-136, 240, 251-252, 255-256, 264
Financial resource, 134
Financial value inventory tracking, 238
Financing, 50, 58, 140
Fixtures, 260-262
Flagstick, 64, 80
Fleet manager, 48, 51-52, 58
Fleet supervisor, 48
Flex point, 25-26, 162
Flexibility, 5-6, 14, 230, 306
Flight laws, 31-32
Floor layout, 260
Flop shot, 287-288
Flo-swing concept, 29-30
Fluffy lie, 284
Focus group, 146
Folded merchandise, 262
Follow the leader, 250
Follow through, 294
Food and beverage director, 312
Food and beverage operation, 309-310, 312, 314, 316, 328
Food and beverage regulations, 327-328
Food and beverage service levels, 319-320
Food and beverage staffing level, 319-322
Food cost control, 313-314
Food cost goal, 316
Force, 27-28, 30, 40
Forearms, 24, 302
Four-ball match play, 64
Four-ball stroke play, 66
Foursomes, 64
Fringe benefit, 115-116
Full maintenance fixed rate lease, 56
Functional resume, 124
Fungicide, 190, 196
Fungus, 196

G

Gene Sarazan, 290
General manager, 93-94
GEODE model, 149-150
Golf ball, 8, 10, 12, 17-18, 21-22, 28, 31-32, 71-72, 163-166, 168, 236, 282, 288, 304
Golf ball diameter, 72
Golf ball flight laws, 31-32
Golf ball material, 164, 166
Golf ball performance, 165-166
Golf ball specifications, 71-72
Golf ball weight, 72, 164

Golf car, 43-60, 90, 94, 96, 212, 222
Golf car acquisition, 48, 52, 57-58
Golf car dealer, 49-50
Golf car expenses, 47-48
Golf car fleet, 47-48, 51-54, 57-60, 94
Golf car fleet manager, 48, 51-52, 58
Golf car fleet size, 53-54
Golf car fleet staff, 47-48
Golf car lease, 55-56
Golf car maintenance, 48, 52, 58-60
Golf car model, 49-50
Golf car rental, 44, 46
Golf car repair, 52, 60
Golf car revenue, 43-46
Golf car storage, 48, 52-54, 60, 212
Golf clinic, 158, 303-304
Golf club components, 15-16
Golf club evaluation, 159-160
Golf course design, 197-212, 215-222
Golf course renovation, 140, 223-224
Golf course routing, 204-206, 219-220
Golf course traffic, 221-222
Golf facility evaluation, 89-90
Golf facility types, 305-310
Golf hole types, 223-224
Golf industry trends, 134, 240, 242
Golf knowledge, 156-158
Golf range, 91-92, 94, 168
Golf shop, 92, 94, 138, 232, 236, 242, 244, 246, 252, 260, 262-264
Golf shop maintenance, 263-264
Golf swing learning model, 103-104
Golf technology, 224
Grading, 208, 210
Grain, 281-282
Graphite shaft, 161-162
Grease spot, 196
Green contour, 216
Green construction, 215-216
Greenside bunker, 290-294
Grip, 16, 18, 23-24, 36, 279-280, 284, 288, 302
Grip placement, 24
Grip precision, 24
Grip pressure, 24, 284
Grip strength, 24
Grip types, 23-24
Gross margin, 132, 248, 251-252

Gross margin return on investment (GMROI), 251-252
Ground under repair, 77-78
Group lesson, 301-302
Grow-in phase (Phase IV), 198, 200, 211-212
Growing point, 176

H

Handicap, 30, 81-82, 96
Hanging merchandise, 262
Hard good, 234
Hazard, 64, 74, 77-80, 208, 217-218
Head professional, 94-96, 138
Health care coverage, 116
Health insurance, 116
Heavy equipment operator, 210
Heel, 18, 292
Herbicide, 190, 198
Heroic golf hole, 224
Hiring, 96, 118, 120, 138, 168, 201-204, 209-210, 321-322
Hiring process, 321-322
Historical site, 206
Hitting behind ball, 290
Honorary President, 88
Hook, 8, 290
Hosel, 4, 10
Human resource, 270
Humidity, 326
Hydrologist, 202

I

Identifying ball, 64
Immigration Reform and Control Act (IRCA), 120
Immovable obstruction, 73-74
Impact, 8, 10, 12, 26, 36, 166, 168
Impact location, 166
Income, 114, 140, 310
Independent contractor, 88
Ingredients, 318
Initial velocity, 164
Input, 104, 267-268
Insect prevention, 191-192
Insecticide, 190, 192, 196
Insects, 76, 190-194
Inside takeaway, 34
Instructor, 34, 102, 105-108, 155-158, 276, 278, 304
Instructor feedback, 105-106
Instructor traits, 155-156
In-swing principles, 35-36
Intangible asset, 138

Integrated Pest Management (IPM), 191-192
Interior designer, 204
Interlocking grip, 24
Internal drainage, 214
Interpersonal skills, 151-152
Interview, 121-122, 160, 322
Interviewing, 322
Inventory, 90, 230-238, 252-256, 260-262, 311-312, 326
Inventory level, 90, 230, 232, 237-238, 254
Inventory management method, 326
Inventory tracking system, 237-238
Inventory turnover rate, 232, 235-236, 238, 252, 256
Iron shot, 167-168, 292
Irrigation, 208, 210-212
Irrigation specialist, 210
Irrigation system, 211-212

J

Job loss, 256
Joint problem solving, 274

K

Keystoning, 246
Kinesiology, 37-38
Kinesthetic golfer, 30, 102
Kinesthetic learning method, 102
Kitchen, 314

L

Land, 202, 214
Land planner, 202
Landscape architect, 204
Landscaping, 208
Lateral water hazard, 64, 79-80
Lawsuit, 328
Lead tape, 4, 6
Lease/purchase, 56
Leasing, 55-56
Left-handed golfer, 303-304
Legal counsel, 202
Length of arc, 31-32, 36
Lessee, 56
Lesson, 90, 157-158, 301-302
Lessons per day, 157-158
Lessor, 56
Lever system, 19-20, 36, 282
Leverage, 14, 30
Lie angle, 10

Life insurance, 116
Lift, 28, 64
Ligament, 37-38
Lighting, 260
Lime, 180
Line of play, 62, 218
Linear trend analysis, 135-136
Liquor, 326-328
Liquor license, 328
Liquor service, 326-328
Litigation, 114
Loam soil, 178
Local rules, 66
Loft, 9-12, 280
Loose impediment, 64, 75-76
Lost ball, 64
Low handicap, 30

M

Maintenance, 48, 52, 56, 58-60, 168, 186, 198, 200, 214
Maintenance phase (Phase V), 198, 200
Maintenance staff, 168
Maintenance supervisor, 48
Manufacturer's suggested retail price, 246
Market demand, 224, 240, 250
Market trend, 240
Markup, 245-250
Master key, 109-110
Match play, 62, 64, 68
Mechanic, 48
Men's apparel, 232
Menu, 314-316, 318
Menu concept, 316
Menu cost, 316
Menu development, 315-316
Merchandise, 90, 96, 146, 229-240, 244-246, 253-254, 258, 261-262, 266
Merchandise assortment plan (MAP), 230, 239-240
Merchandise classification, 230-232, 240
Merchandise inventory level, 90
Merchandise sales, 90
Merchandising, 96, 229-230
Merchandising steps, 229-230
Merger clause, 112
Mesomorph, 298-300
Military service, 120, 124
Mill River Plan, 246
Minimum wage, 120
Minors, 118
Mission statement, 129-130, 276

Mole crickets, 194
Moment of truth, 145-146
Monetary fine, 68, 328
Motion, 38, 40, 64, 302
Motivation, 105-106, 130, 156, 271-274
Motor function, 40
Mound, 220
Movable obstruction, 73-74
Mowing, 185-188, 198
Mowing frequency, 187-188
Mowing height, 186-188, 198
Muscle, 38-40, 42, 298, 300
Muscular endurance, 306

N

National Director of PGA, 90
National officer of PGA, 90
Natural feature, 218
Natural object, 76
Natural resource, 138
Nematodes, 194
Net total value, 132
Networking, 125-126
Neuromuscular coordination, 14, 39-40
9-hole golf course, 92
Nitrogen, 170, 182

Non-compete clause, 112
Northern climate grass, 173-174
Nutrient, 169-170, 176, 178, 184, 196

O

Obstructions, 64, 73-74
Occupational Safety and Health Act (OSHA), 120, 168
One-lever stroke, 282
One-lever swing, 20
Open clubface, 12, 286
Open-to-buy (OTB) plan, 230-232, 260
Operating expense, 48
Operational budget, 140
Operational goal, 308
Opportunistic pricing, 250
Orange stakes, 78
Order of play, 62
Organizational structure, 94, 142
Orientation, 322-324
Original cost, 132
Out of bounds, 64, 220
Over swing, 296
Overall distance, 164
Overhead cost, 258
Overlapping grip, 24
Overseeding, 172, 185-186
Overtime pay, 120

P

P-A-C-E, 311-312
Par, 66
Par-3, 218
Par stock, 312
Parking area, 92, 168, 212
Participation clinic, 304
Parts and service, 50, 56
Pay period, 324
Payroll, 310
Peak season, 238
Penal golf hole, 224
Pension, 114
Performance analysis, 135-136
Performance formulas, 131-132
Performance indicator, 251-252
Performance standards, 142
Permanent markdown, 253-254
Permit, 328
Perpetual book inventory tracking, 238
Personal use of golf facility, 116
Pest, 189-192
Pest categories, 189-190
Pest control, 189-190
PGA Apprentice, 84, 97-98
PGA Board of Control, 88-90
PGA Board of Directors, 87-88, 100
PGA Constitution, 83-86
PGA credit union, 58
PGA District, 88, 97-98
PGA employment services, 121-122
PGA head professional, 94-96, 138
PGA member rights, 99-100
PGA membership status, 99-100
PGA of America, 83-84
PGA officer, 87-88, 90
PGA President, 88, 90
PGA recognized golf course, 91-92, 216
PGA recognized golf range, 91-92
PGA Section, 68, 90, 97-98
PGA teaching triangle, 101-102
PGA Tour, 84
PGA Vice President, 88
Phase I: Site analysis, 198, 200-202
Phase II: Design, 198, 200, 203-204, 206, 208
Phase III: Development, 198, 200, 209-210

Phase IV: Grow-in, 198, 200, 211-212
Phase V: Maintenance, 198, 200
Phosphorous, 170, 182
Physical strength, 14, 158
Physical unit inventory tracking, 238
Picture board, 313-314
Pitch, 281-284
Planogram, 243-244
Plant, 175-176, 178, 184, 196-198
Plant root, 175-176, 184, 196
Plant shoot, 175-176
Plant structure, 198
Planting preparation, 210
Play ball as it lies, 64, 80
Playing Ability Test (PAT), 98
Playing fees, 44
Point-of-sale (POS) system, 259-260
Point-of-sale markdown, 254
Policies and procedures, 52, 94, 141-142, 324
Policy, 52, 94, 112, 141-142, 324, 327-328
Political landscape, 202
Pond, 220
Pore space, 180
Portion cost, 316, 318
Portion size, 318
Positional swing concept, 29-30
Posture, 40
Potassium, 170, 182
Practice, 62, 168, 206, 283-284
Practice facility, 206
Practice putting green, 168
Practice shot routine, 283-284
Preparing food, 314, 318
Pressure, 24, 284
Pre-swing principles, 35-36
Preventative maintenance, 60
Price, 50, 230, 234-242, 246-250, 254-258, 260, 314, 316
Price control, 260
Price multiplier, 316
Price point, 240
Pricing, 236, 242, 246, 250, 255-258
Private golf facility, 236, 248, 306-310
Privately managed golf facility, 308-310
Probation, 86
Procedures, 52, 86, 94, 141-144, 278, 318, 324
Product availability, 250
Product consistency, 318

Professional affiliations, 124
Professional development points (PDPs), 100
Profit, 130, 132, 240, 248, 252, 258, 308, 310
Profit goal, 258
Profitability, 130, 240, 252
Promotional event, 265-266
Provisional ball, 64
Public golf facility, 248, 306
Publicist, 204
Pull, 290
Purchase order (PO), 257-258
Purchasing, 230, 312, 314
Push, 290
Putter characteristics, 279-280
Putter length, 280
Putter lie, 280
Putter loft, 280
Putter weight, 280
Putting green, 64, 73-74, 168, 172, 188, 208, 214-216, 220, 222
Putting grip, 279-280
Putting principles, 277-278
Pythium blight, 196

Q

Quality, 130, 146, 148, 160
Quality of service, 130

R

Range of motion, 38, 302
Rate of movement, 44
Recipe, 316-318
Record keeping, 57-58, 60, 120
Recreational golf experience, 225-226
Recruiting, 96, 322
Regulations, 85-86, 327-328
Regulatory trends, 134
Rehearse golf swing, 284
Reinforced problem solving, 274
Release, 36
Religious affiliations, 124
Renovations, 140, 223-224
Repair, 52, 60, 78, 96
Reputation, 50
Resale value, 56
Resources, 134, 138, 144, 202, 206, 267-270
Résumés, 122-124
Retail price, 246, 248
Retail sales, 132, 234, 252
Retain staff, 323-324

Retirement plan, 114, 116
Revenue, 43-46, 132, 136, 252
Revenue per round, 252
Rhythm, 43-44
Right to hold office, 100
Right to vote, 100
Right-handed golfer, 220, 304
Right-of-way, 206
Rights of PGA members, 99-100
Root, 175-176, 184, 196
Root zone, 184
Rotation, 24, 42, 58, 280, 302
Rough, 188, 222
Rounds played, 54, 90, 132, 136
Routing, 204-206, 219-220
Routing plan, 204-206
Royal and Ancient Golf Club (R&A), 71-72
Rule violation, 67-68, 85-86
Rules Drafting Committee, 70
Rules of golf, 61-66, 69-70, 72
Ryegrass, 174

S

Safety, 54, 120, 168, 219-220
Sales goals, 236
Sales volume, 256, 258
Sand, 294, 296
Sand wedge, 289-290
Sandy soil, 178, 180
Sanitation, 326
Savings and loan, 58
Schematic, 206
Seasonal staff, 168
Sectional officer, 90
Selling process, 265-266
Seminar, 158
Semi-private golf facility, 306
Semi-private lesson, 302
Senior golfer, 301-302
Sequence of movements, 44
Setup, 36
Shaft, 4-6, 8, 10, 12, 16, 18, 26, 161-162
Shaft flexibility, 4-6, 25-26, 162
Shelter, 212
Shipping and handling, 234
Shirts, 236
Shoes, 232, 252
Shoot, 175-176
Shoulder turn, 42
Side wind, 296
Sidehill lie, 290
Signage, 260
Site analysis phase (Phase I), 198, 200-202

Sizing merchandise, 261-262
Skeletal structure, 40, 42
Skill level, 305-306
Skip payment lease, 56
Slice, 220, 290
Slope, 214, 216
Snow, 172
Social affiliations, 124
Sod webworms, 194
Soft good, 234
Soil, 177-180, 184, 196, 198, 214
Soil amendment, 214
Soil classification, 177-178
Soil compaction, 179-180, 198
Soil content, 177-178, 184, 214
Soil pH, 179-180
Sole, 10, 12, 15-16, 288, 290, 292
Sole inversion, 15-16, 290
Southern climate grass, 173-174
Spring dating, 244
Square clubface, 12, 16, 278, 288
Stableford competition, 66
Staff, 47-48, 60, 96, 134, 141-142, 144, 168, 260, 316, 319-324
Staff orientation, 322-324
Staff resources, 134
Staff scheduling, 96
Staff selling skills, 260
Staff training, 60
Staffing, 141-142, 144, 319-322
Stakes, 78
Staking, 210
Stale merchandise, 254
Standard plate presentation, 314
Standard portion cost, 316, 318
Standard recipe, 317-318
Starting, 96
Steel shaft, 161-162
Stock option, 114
Stock outage, 242
Storage cost, 48
Storage space, 54, 60
Storeroom, 314, 325-326
Strategic golf hole, 224
Strength, 14, 24, 130, 158, 162, 300, 302, 306
Stretch reflex, 41-42
Stroke play, 62, 66, 68
Substituted ball, 64
Subsurface drainage, 213-214
Subsurface insects, 193-194
Sulfur, 180
Superintendent, 167-168, 192, 200

Supply and demand, 224, 240, 250
Surface drainage, 213-214
Surface insects, 193-194
Survey, 146, 284
Suspension, 68, 86
Swing center, 36
Swing error, 106, 109-110
Swing path, 22, 28, 32, 166
Swing plane, 19-20, 36
Swing preference, 33-34
Swing weight, 3-4, 6, 14
SWOT analysis, 129-130
Symmetry of design pattern, 164
Syringing, 181-182

T

Tagging, 242
Takeaway, 34
Tangible asset, 138
Targeted resume, 124
Task-relationship connection, 147-148
Tax basis, 138
Taxes, 120, 138
Teaching aid, 107-108
Teaching approach, 277-278
Teaching drill, 109-110
Teaching goal, 107-108
Teaching philosophy, 275-276, 278
Teaching triangle, 101-102
Technology, 224
Tee area, 64, 74, 92, 188, 208, 212, 214, 217-218, 220, 222
Tee marker, 212, 222
Tee times, 96
Temperature, 172, 326
Tempo, 43-44
Temporary markdown, 253-254
Tendon, 37-38
Ten-finger grip, 24
Tensile strength, 162
Termination clause, 112
Terrain, 52, 284
Test recipe, 316
Thatch, 192, 195-196
Three-ball, 64
Threesomes, 64
Through the green, 73-74
Time-based resource, 270
Timing, 36, 43-44
Toe, 8, 292, 294
Topdressing, 183-184
Topography, 214
Topsoil Greens Construction Method, 216
Torque, 7-8, 162
Total course area, 92
Total retail sales, 132, 234, 252
Tournament officials, 82

Tournament operations, 96
Tournament pairing sheet, 81-82
Trade-in value, 46, 50
Traffic, 221-222
Trail fees, 46
Training, 60, 96, 324
Trajectory, 10, 17-18, 20, 26, 28, 284
Transition zone, 170
Trees, 220
Turfgrass, 168-174, 176, 180, 182, 186, 192, 194-196, 198, 282
Turfgrass adaptation, 169-170
Turfgrass disease, 176, 190, 195-196
Turfgrass management program, 168
Turfgrass zones, 169-170
Turnover, 232, 235-236, 238, 252, 256
Two-lever stroke, 282
Two-lever swing, 20

U

"U" shaped swing, 292
Uneven lie, 289-290
United States Golf Association (USGA), 70-72, 216
Unpaid taxes, 120
Unplayable ball, 64
Uphill lie, 290
Use of PGA name and logo, 100
USGA, 70-72, 216
USGA Greens Construction Method, 216
USGA Rules Committee, 70
Utilities, 202, 206

V

"V" shaped swing, 292
Vegetable weevils, 194
Velocity, 164
Vendor, 230, 234, 241-242, 244, 328
Ventilation, 54
Verbal learning method, 102
Veterans Rights and Military Service Act, 120
Visual golfer, 30, 102, 284
Visual golfer learning method, 102
Visualize shot, 284
Volume of sand, 294

W - Z

Wall thickness, 162
Warm season grass, 170, 186

Warranty, 50, 56
Water hazard, 64, 78
Watering, 182, 194, 198
Weather, 52, 134
Wedge, 289-290
Weeds, 190, 192, 197-198
Weight, 3-6, 14, 42, 164, 180, 280
White grubs, 194
White lines, 78
Wholesale price, 234
Width of arc, 31-32, 36
Wind, 295-296
Wind against, 296
Women's apparel, 232
Wood, 11-12
Work conditions, 272
Work environment, 120, 271-272
Work status, 120
Worms, 76, 194
Wristiness, 280
Wrists, 20, 24, 26, 280, 282, 288
Wrong ball, 64
Yardage, 52
Yellow lines, 78
Yellow stakes, 78
Young golfers, 24
Zoysiagrass, 174

www.ingramcontent.com/pod-product-compliance
Lightning Source LLC
LaVergne TN
LVHW051037080426
835508LV00019B/1570